Aida

Aida

GIUSEPPI VERDI

TEXT BY DAVID FOIL

BLACK DOG
& LEVENTHAL
PUBLISHERS
NEW YORK

Published by
Black Dog & Leventhal Publishers, Inc.
151 West 19th Street
New York, NY 10011

Distributed by
Workman Publishing Company
708 Broadway
New York, NY 10003

Designed by Alleycat Design, Inc.

Series editor: Judith Dupré

Book manufactured in Singapore

ISBN: 1-884822-80-0

h g f

FOREWORD

*A*ida is the opera that has it all. The story is exciting. The music is splendid and, from start to finish, memorably melodic. And the epic, cast-of-thousands sprawl of the drama is so vividly caught in Verdi's score that you can literally see its splendor simply by listening. This is what grand opera is all about. But the ultimate grandeur in Aida is the supreme genius of Verdi, experienced here in peak form.

You will hear the entire opera on the two compact discs included on the inside front and back covers of this book. As you explore the book, you will discover the story behind the opera and its creation, the background of the composer, biographies of the principal singers and conductor, and the opera's text, or libretto, both in the original Italian and in an English translation. Special commentary has been included throughout the libretto to aid in your appreciation and highlight key moments in the action and the score.

Enjoy this book and enjoy the music.

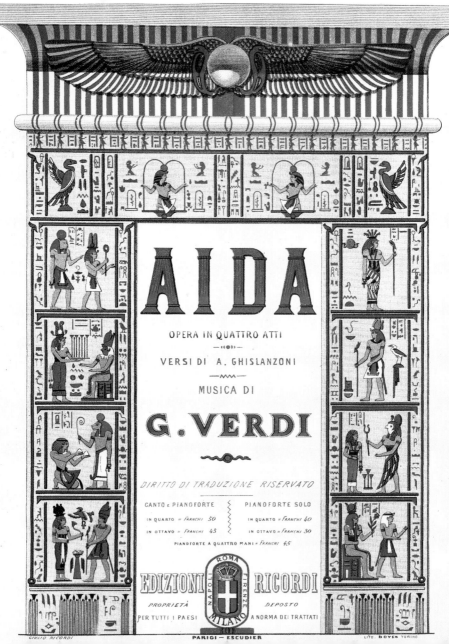

Aida

It was the letter Camille du Locle had long awaited. For three years, the French producer had conducted a patient correspondence with the celebrated composer Giuseppe Verdi concerning the possibility of a new opera. Du Locle was interested in having such an opera for Paris, where Verdi's most recent work, *Don Carlos* (on which du Locle had collaborated), had been produced three years earlier. Du Locle's agenda was complicated; he was also operating as an intermediary for a respected French Egyptologist named Auguste Mariette (known by the noble title Mariette Bey, later Mariette Pasha) and Mariette's friend, the khedive of Egypt. The khedive had long been obsessed with the idea of having Verdi write an opera especially for his new opera house in Cairo, and he had crafted with Mariette an outline of an operatic plot. It concerned the story of an enslaved Ethiopian princess, Aida, who loved the Egyptian captain Radamès, who had conquered her homeland and was himself the object of desire of Aida's jealous mistress, the Egyptian princess Amneris.

"I have read the Egyptian outline," Verdi wrote from his country home Sant'Agata, near Busseto, Italy, on May 26, 1870. "It is well done; it offers a splendid *mise-en-scène,* and there are two or three situations which, if not very new, are certainly very beautiful. . . . Now let's hear the financial conditions from Egypt, and then we shall decide." Verdi went on to ask some questions about the outline and wondered who would fashion the Italian libretto. In the same letter, he told du Locle to halt plans to translate the Spanish drama *d'Ayala,* which had interested him as a possible opera subject. So it was clear to du Locle that a decision had been made: "the Egyptian outline" was shaping up as the next Verdi opera. Du Locle considered Verdi's response an enthusiastic one, and he knew the khedive would reply with an ample and attractive offer. The details quickly fell into place, work began immediately, and, despite the interference of the Franco-Prussian War

GIUSEPPE VERDI (1813–1901)

and the relentless perfectionism of Verdi himself, on December 24, 1871, the curtain of the Cairo Opera House rose on the opera "the Egyptian outline" had become: *Aida.*

Aida tells a remarkable story, one that has inspired a book of nearly seven hundred pages, Hans Busch's highly readable and indispensable *Verdi's Aida: The History of an Opera in Letters and Documents.* Nowhere in that book, however, will you find any confirmation of the widespread myth that Verdi wrote

SANT'AGATA, VERDI'S COUNTRY HOME.

Aida, at the khedive's request, to celebrate the opening of the Suez Canal. The source of that legend can probably be found in the khedive's ardent desire to commission an opera from Verdi, his favorite composer. He seems to have approached the composer to write something—possibly nothing more than a celebratory hymn—for the opening of the Cairo Opera House in 1869. The opera house was indeed built to celebrate the opening of the Suez Canal, but Verdi did not accept any commission from the khedive at that time; in fact, correspondence from the

THE ROYAL OPERA HOUSE IN CAIRO.

khedive seems to have been handled by Verdi's wife, Giuseppina. The opera that opened the Cairo theater on November 1, 1869, was indeed one of Verdi's—the eighteen-year-old *Rigoletto*—but the composer seems not to have concerned himself with the occasion. The Suez Canal itself did not open until almost a month later, several months before Verdi received the outline that would win for the khedive the privilege of commissioning a new Verdi opera.

When Verdi received du Locle's proposal in the spring of 1870, he was, at the age of fifty-six, the world's most acclaimed and successful opera composer. Not only had his work earned him enduring international acclaim, he was adored as a patriot-hero in his native Italy, which was then struggling with the task of national unification. Verdi had written operas for Paris *(Les Vêpres Siciliennes* and *Don Carlos)*, London *(I masnadieri)*, and St. Petersburg *(La forza del destino)*, as well as for all the principal theaters in Italy. Every major opera house in the world performed his work. At this point, the highlights of his career included, in addition to the operas mentioned above, *Nabucodonosor (Nabucco)*, *Ernani*, *Macbeth*, *Luisa Miller*, *Rigoletto*, *La traviata*, *Il trovatore*, *Simon Boccanegra*, and *Un ballo in maschera.*

Still, he endured his share of failures and setbacks. Possibly because he was concerned about the indifferent response Parisian audiences had given *Don Carlos* when it premiered in 1867, Verdi had resisted for three years after that a constant stream of offers and proposals for new operas, even though he had reached a point in his career where he could write anything he wanted and make any deal he wished; whatever he chose to do, his publisher, the formidable house of Ricordi, would support and serve him.

Founded in 1808 by an enterprising music copyist named Giovanni Ricordi, the firm of G. Ricordi & Company became the behind-the-scenes power in Italian music in the nineteenth and early twentieth century. Giovanni Ricordi's friendship with Gioacchino Rossini established the firm, and Ricordi's early recognition of Verdi's genius cemented its position. The next three generations of Ricordi sons—Tito, Giulio (who discovered Giacomo Puccini), and Tito—carried on the family tradition of discovering talented composers, aggressively publishing and advocating their work and generally keeping a hawklike watch on company interests as well as those of its clients.

These circumstances, however, would not stir Verdi into action in the late 1860s. His letters reveal how offended he was by the reception accorded *Don Carlos,* an opera he would eventually revise and have translated into Italian. Why would Verdi have been so upset about an indifferent reaction from a bourgeois audience in Paris? To understand that is to understand why Verdi wanted to write operas for Paris, as well as what the term "grand opera" means, and the long tradition from which *Aida* emerged.

Grand opera is exactly what it sounds like—opera performed on a grand scale. Cultivated to appeal to the tastes of a newly enfranchised middle-class Parisian audience, grand opera had become a virtual genre by the early nineteenth century. It built on an aesthetic style that had flourished with Napoléon and his followers, and was an exercise in sensory overload that emphasized spectacle and splendor, usually in the context of a sprawling and lofty story with a historical setting. Casts were huge and productions were lavishly ornamented with ballet sequences and monumental stage tableaux, not unlike the Hollywood blockbuster films of a century later.

It was the Italian composer Rossini who originated the concept of grand opera while writing for Paris. Rossini premiered his last opera, *Guillaume Tell* (William Tell), in Paris in 1829 at a time when audiences were apparently ready for its innovations. Not only did *Guillaume Tell* have a monumental scale (and length), its superbly integrated score achieved a magnificence equal to the eye-popping spectacle unfolding onstage.

Guillaume Tell became the prototype for grand opera, a movement that would find its master in the German-born émigré known to Parisian audiences as Giacomo Meyerbeer (1791–1864). Meyerbeer was the composer of *Le Prophète, Les Huguenots, Robert le diable,* and *L'Africaine,* operas rarely performed

VERDI CONDUCTING AIDA.

A 1908 PRODUCTION
OF AIDA AT THE
METROPOLITAN
OPERA.

GRAND OPERA TRADITIONALLY FEATURED LAVISH PRODUCTIONS, AS SEEN IN THIS SETTING OF THE TRIUMPHAL SCENE AT THE METROPOLITAN OPERA.

today, despite passages of beauty and grace, because they are unconscionably long, almost absurdly preoccupied with spectacle, and inconsistent in their musical quality. For these very reasons, Paris audiences loved Meyerbeer's operas. Going to the opera was a social occasion as well as a cultural one, and Meyerbeer's operas, with as many as five substantial acts, afforded many intermissions for socializing. And when Parisians turned their attention to the stage, Meyerbeer saw to it that they were dazzled, and often. His skillful music seemed to spring from nothing more profound than his desire to please his singers and tickle the ears of his audiences. There is, however, a vast gulf between cleverness and art. To listeners who have experienced grand opera as conceived by Verdi, Richard Wagner, and even Puccini, Meyerbeer's pleasant melodies and his taste for bombast can sound mindless and empty. Both he and his operas were overwhelmingly popular yet derided by sophisticated observers, much in the same way Andrew Lloyd Webber's musicals are today.

RICHARD WAGNER AND VERDI BOTH LONGED TO EMULATE THE GRAND OPERAS OF GIACOMO MEYERBEER.

Wagner, who professed to despise both Meyerbeer and his music, longed to emulate him and did. And Verdi twice attempted to write Meyerbeer-like grand operas for Paris. Neither composer succeeded at first because each was more than a mere entertainer; indeed, it seemed as if they were working in another art form altogether. When Wagner tried to introduce *Tannhäuser* to Parisian audiences in 1861, he ensured an outright disaster by refusing to place the de rigueur ballet sequence (which he had willingly provided for Paris) in the second act to accommodate the members of the elite

Jockey Club, many of whom had mistresses in the corps de ballet, and who pre-
ferred to dine during the first act. The coolness with which Paris greeted Verdi's
Les Vêpres Siciliennes and *Don Carlos*—both of which contain some of his subtlest
and most inspired writing, especially the latter,—suggests only that Verdi had
not pitched his work to a sufficiently low common denominator. Verdi eventually
saw to it that both operas were translated into Italian. Once embraced by a more
sympathetic audience in Verdi's homeland, the two works are now remembered
by their Italian titles, *I vespri siciliani* and *Don Carlo.*

"It is neither the labor of writing an opera nor the judgment of the Parisian
public that holds me back, but rather the certainty of not being able to have my
music performed in Paris the way I want it," Verdi wrote in a long letter to du
Locle after the *Don Carlos* premiere, voicing his frustrations with the prejudices
and intrigues of the Paris Opéra. "It is quite singular that an author must always
see his ideas frustrated and his conceptions distorted! In your opera houses—I
say this without the slightest sarcasm—there are too many know-it-alls!
Everyone wants to judge according to their own ideas, their own tastes, and,
what is worse, according to a system, without taking into account the character
and the individuality of the author. . . . I don't mean to disapprove of what you
people do; I only mean to tell you that it is absolutely impossible for me to subject
myself again . . . to your theaters, when I know that a true success is not possible
for me unless I write as I feel, free from any influence and without considering
that I am writing for Paris rather than the world of the moon."

Grand opera began to lose its vogue after Meyerbeer's death, its demise
hastened as Verdi and Wagner offered striking alternatives to its mere pomp and
circumstance. Because of this, it is interesting that Verdi chose to refer to the
Meyerbeer model one last time with *Aida,* almost as if he wished to prove that

THE DOME
OF THE
PARIS
OPÉRA.

AN ENORMOUS BLUE SCARAB ADORNS DOUGLAS SCHMIDT'S 1981 PRODUCTION
DESIGN FOR THE SAN FRANCISCO OPERA.

he could get it right. He did a good deal more than that, creating what is surely
the finest grand opera of them all and one of his absolute masterpieces.

Aida's greatness lies not simply in Verdi's grasp of spectacle but in his ability
to tell, in musical terms, a powerful human drama that is also startling in its
intimacy. Aside from the triumphal scene in Act II, the great moments in *Aida*
are intensely personal ones, even though they are set in a spectacular context.
The conclusion of the first scene of Act I, for instance, begins with an impressive,

strutting, Meyerbeer-like ensemble that issues a stirring call to war with the words "Ritorna vincitor!" (return victorious!), which the title character echoes ironically when she is left alone to examine her dilemma. Yet the final moments of the scene are not brassy and public but vulnerable and private—Aida weeps softly and begs the gods for deliverance.

As generous as the inspiration and flow of melody are in *Aida,* it is the economy of means and the discriminating choices Verdi made —in the text as well as the music—that transform a sprawling and tuneful spectacle into a masterpiece. He wastes no time, plunging the audience into the heart of the drama mere minutes into the action, when Radamès professes his love for Aida. Within twenty minutes of his aria—in richly melodic music driven by the most vivid and expressive momentum— we have met Amneris, witnessed

AIDA CONTAINS POWERFUL YET INTIMATE MOMENTS IN SCENES SUCH AS THIS ONE BETWEEN THE KNEELING AIDA (NINA RAUTIO) AND AMNERIS (DELORA ZAJIK).

MUSICAL
MANUSCRIPT
OF AIDA.

her realization that she is the "other woman," seen a war break out that will affect each of the characters, and discovered Aida's secret.

The composer chose as his Italian librettist Antonio Ghislanzoni, who had won his confidence in assisting with the revisions of *La forza del destino* for its La Scala premiere in 1869. Once the khedive's commission for *Aida* had been accepted—for a fee so lavish that even Verdi was nervous about the amount becoming public knowledge—Verdi and his wife made an Italian translation of Mariette's outline, and the composer added extensive preliminary notes about dialogue. The actual writing and basic composition of *Aida* took only a few months after the composer and librettist met face to face in mid-July of 1870, after which Verdi inaugurated a blizzard of correspondence with Ghislanzoni to get exactly the libretto—with precisely the verses—he imagined.

Verdi was adamant about the tiniest details, from the poetic meter of a line and how its stresses affected a musical phrase to the selection of words that would not detract from the musical flow. He asked for revisions repeatedly to hone the text to its leanest and most insightful expression, and to make it as lucid as it was concise. He wanted the libretto to speak so clearly that he, as the composer, could amplify its more profound meaning through the music so that the audience would have no trouble understanding what was sung and where the story was going, while the musical treatment shaped a deeper awareness of the drama's poetry.

While *Aida* was being written, France declared war on Prussia, a development that exasperated Verdi (who sympathized with the French despite his contempt for the arrogance of the Second Empire) and intensified his strong nationalistic feelings, which would be reflected in the character of Aida herself. The war ended in a matter of months, but it derailed the timetable established for *Aida's* premiere since du Locle and Mariette were in a besieged Paris and production plans could not be finalized, nor could the designs for the scenery and costumes, which were being created in Paris. Verdi continued to demand revisions from Ghislanzoni. Ultimately, the delay caused by the Franco-Prussian War allowed Verdi the luxury of orchestrating his score at his own pace and planning the stage production in comprehensive detail. Although Verdi informed his publisher Giulio Ricordi that he had finished composing the opera in November 1870 (and wondered how he could get the rest of the fee due him), Ricordi was presented with the finished product in August 1871.

EARLY COSTUME SKETCH FOR THE CHARACTER OF RADAMÈS.

The composer did not attend the world premiere in Cairo on Christmas eve of 1871, joking in a letter to a friend that he was afraid of being "mummi-fied." Although a boatload of dignitaries from Italy did make the trip, Verdi steadfastly refused to join them. His reasons for not going are unclear—it is known that he was a guarded, intensely private man—although his absence may have had to do with his greater interest in *Aida's* Italian premiere at La Scala a month later. Verdi, who was involved with every aspect of this production, com-posed a full-scale *Aida* overture for the occasion that he immediately and wise-ly discarded in favor of the brief, ethereal prelude he had originally written. (Both Arturo Toscanini and Claudio Abbado have recorded the alternate *Aida* overture, which runs a little over ten minutes and seeks to encapsulate the drama; the opera does not need it.) The Cairo premiere was a triumph, but from all reports the first performance at La Scala far outshone the Egyptian pro-duction. Thunderous ovations greeted arias and ensembles within the opera. Verdi was hailed once again as a national hero and was presented with a baton bearing his name encrusted in precious jewels. Typically, he kept a veteran's level head about the excitement, this time with a self-effacement that was almost comical. "The audience reacted favorably," he wrote to a friend in early February 1872, just after the La Scala opening, adding, "I don't want to affect modesty with you, but this opera is certainly not one of my worst."

Aida has remained at the forefront of the international repertoire ever since its premiere, despite the fact that it is an expensive and demanding opera to stage and perform. As with other Verdi operas of this period, the score's rich-ness and scale of expression push lyric singers to a more forceful and heroic kind of utterance—the Italian word *spinto* ("pushed") is often used to describe this kind of singing. The score is especially challenging in *Aida,* in which larger-than-

IN 1925, AIDA WAS PRESENTED OUTDOORS AT EBBET'S FIELD, BROOKLYN, NEW YORK.

life public moments contrast suddenly with intimate, private ones. Lyric singers who lack stamina and solid techniques have come to grief in the opera's four leading roles, while other singers, though heroic, may lack the tenderness and vulnerability that are crucial to the characters. The performers heard on this recording are especially successful in fully encompassing their roles.

Listen, for instance, to Franco Corelli's thrilling performance of the aria "Celeste Aida," which he caps with a dazzling high B-flat that he immediately scales back to an ardent pianissimo—an effect Verdi requested in his score but that few tenors are capable of delivering comfortably. The aria comes within a few minutes of the opera's opening—a rude jolt to a tenor who must deliver his big moment without much of a warm-up onstage. In fact, the most popular tenor of the pre-Caruso era, Jean deReszke, routinely cut "Celeste Aida" if he did not feel like singing it! Verdi, ever the pragmatist, devised an alternative for an overwhelmed tenor: instead of having to hold the B-flat (with or without the diminuendo), he had the tenor hit the high note and immediately drop an octave to repeat the phrase.

Aida herself has a similar precarious moment in Act III, known as the Nile scene, in which the heroine secretly meets Radamès at night on the banks of the Nile. She sings an exquisite, introspective aria, confronting once again the dilem-

AIDA SINGS "O PATRIA MIA" IN A PRODUCTION DESIGNED BY MICHAEL YEARGEN AT THE SAN DIEGO OPERA.

ma that is tearing her apart. At the penultimate moment, she must twice rise to a high C, in approaches that are difficult and—with Verdi's subtle, even translucent orchestration—leave the voice completely exposed. The Egyptian princess Amneris, Aida's nemesis, must rise to the same remarkable level of intensity in the judgment scene in Act IV, in which she anxiously awaits the decision of the high priests as to whether Radamès will live or die. Her anguish is epic, heightened by the guilt she feels for wishing the worst for the lovers, and Verdi crowns it with a shattering high B-flat that demands a lot of any mezzo-soprano who sings the role.

In performance, *Aida* has been seen in venues of virtually every size and shape, from amateur stages to the massive outdoor arenas at Verona and the Baths of Caracalla in Rome. An Italian film of the opera was made in the early 1950s with Sophia Loren in blackface lip-synching the role of Aida. In the style of the popular *Carmen Jones,* in which Georges Bizet's *Carmen* was reset in the pre–Civil War American South, a Broadway musical based on Verdi's score, *My Darlin' Aida,* was staged in 1952, an adaptation that did not succeed. No matter. In its unadulterated form, Verdi's lofty opera has flourished in an unbroken triumph that has now lasted well over a century.

AN OUTDOOR PRODUCTION
OF AIDA IN VERONA, ITALY.

The Story of Aida

ACT I

Scene One

In Memphis, in the palace of the Egyptian king (or pharaoh), a young army captain named Radamès is deep in conversation with the high priest Ramfis. War seems imminent: Ethiopia's army is gathering at Egypt's borders, threatening to descend on the valley of the Nile. The oracle of the goddess Isis has revealed to Ramfis the name of the warrior who will lead Egypt to triumph, a name the king will announce that very day. As the priest departs, Radamès can hardly contain his hope that he will be the chosen general. For only then can he stand before the king and ask to be united with the woman with whom he is secretly in love, the Ethiopian slave princess, Aida. He muses on his love for Aida: he wants to return her to her homeland in triumph and "build her a throne near the sun." Radamès's daydreams are interrupted by the arrival of Amneris, the daughter of the Egyptian king, who, in turn, loves Radamès and tries to tell him about the depth of her feelings for him. But Radamès is distracted, especially when Aida herself suddenly enters. Amneris senses the

A RESPLENDENT RADAMÈS IN A HOUSTON GRAND OPERA PRODUCTION.

unspoken intensity between them. The moment is shattered by the arrival of a messenger with dire news: Amonasro, the Ethiopian king, has invaded Egypt. The king of Egypt immediately declares war and announces that Radamès is indeed the warrior who will lead his armies. The people echo the call for war and implore Radamès to return victorious. As they hurry away, Aida is left alone, wracked with guilt about the inner conflict that is tearing her apart—

Left THE TEMPLE OF VULCAN IN A 1947 PRODUCTION AT THE METROPOLITAN OPERA. *Above* RICHARD TUCKER AS RADAMÈS, IRENE DALIS AS AMNERIS, AND, IN THE CENTER LEONTYNE PRICE AS AIDA.

RADAMÈS (FRANCO CORELLI) ARRIVES IN SPLENDOR.

she is in fact Amonasro's daughter but hopes that Radamès will be victorious—a victory that would destroy her father and homeland but that would unite the two lovers.

During a solemn ceremony in the Temple of Vulcan, priests invoke the aid and protection of the god Phtha. Ramfis presents to Radamès the sacred sword he is to carry into battle, and the young general joins the priests in a passionate prayer for victory.

ACT II

Scene One

The Egyptians have crippled Ethiopia's armies and halted the attack. Radamès is triumphant. In her apartments, Amneris is dressing for her appearance at the victory parade, with which Radamès will return to Memphis to accept the hero's laurel wreath and the king's gratitude. Knowing this is her chance to seize the affection of the young general, Amneris tricks Aida into admitting her love for Radamès and elects to humiliate Aida before Radamès by making her attend the celebration as Amneris's personal slave.

Scene Two

A huge crowd gathers at the gates of Thebes to cheer the arrival of the victorious army. The splendid procession dazzles the grateful crowd, culminating with the arrival of Radamès. The spectacle includes a retinue of Ethiopian prisoners. Aida recognizes among them her father, the king Amonasro, who does not identify

THE TRIUMPHAL
SCENE IN A
PRODUCTION
DESIGNED BY
MICHAEL YEARGEN.

On the **eve of your marriage**, invoke
the **blessing of the goddess Isis.**

AMNERIS AND RAMFIS IN THE TEMPLE OF ISIS IN A SAN DIEGO OPERA PRODUCTION.

himself; claiming instead that Amonasro has actually died in battle, he pleads for mercy for his fellow prisoners. Radamès begs the Egyptian king to release the prisoners, but the king makes a devastating decision: although the prisoners will be freed, Aida and her father will be held as hostages. Grateful for Radamès's triumph, the Egyptian king offers the dismayed general the hand of his daughter, Amneris, ensuring Radamès's future as Egypt's next king.

ACT III

Night descends on the banks of the Nile. Amneris and Ramfis enter the Temple of Isis to pray to the goddess for a blessing on the princess's upcoming marriage. Radamès has sent a message to Aida to meet him at the temple. When she arrives, she finds instead her father. Although Amonasro knows that Aida is in love with his sworn enemy, he pressures her into doing her patriotic duty— namely, coaxing information out of Radamès that will help the Ethiopians in a counterattack. When Radamès arrives, he promises Aida that they will be together once the war has ended. But Aida still fears revenge from Amneris and begs Radamès to run away from Egypt with her. When he reluctantly agrees, she asks him how they can pass through the lines of his own army. He tells her. Amonasro, who has been eavesdropping, steps forward and reveals his identity to the stunned general. Amneris and Ramfis emerge from the temple just as Radamès is pleading with Aida and Amonasro to escape, before surrendering to the guards of the high priest.

ACT IV

Scene One

Although Aida has escaped, Amonasro is dead and Radamès stands accused of treason. Still hoping that her love can save him, Amneris has Radamès brought to her and offers him her assistance if he will renounce Aida. He refuses, telling her that he cannot live without Aida. Amneris listens with mounting hysteria as the priests question Radamès. He says nothing to defend himself, and the priests

THE
JUDGMENT
SCENE.
AMNERIS
BEGS
RADAMÈS
TO SAVE
HIMSELF.

Den
and

charge of treason,
go to the King . . .

have no alternative but to condemn him to death. Amneris tries to intervene, but it is hopeless. She cries in anguish, cursing the authority that is robbing her of the man she loves.

Scene Two

Radamès has been buried alive, sealed in the crypt in the Temple of Vulcan. He discovers in the darkness that Aida is waiting for him: she has stolen into the temple to die with her beloved. As death overtakes them, Aida and Radamès bid farewell to their earthly strife. Above the sealed tomb, Amneris kneels and weeps for Radamès, wishing him peace at long last.

THE FINAL SCENE OF ACT IV
IN A 1988 METROPOLITAN
OPERA PRODUCTION.

The Performers

BIRGIT NILSSON (Aida), perhaps the greatest Wagnerian singer of the last half of the twentieth century, was born in Sweden in 1918 on a small farm near Västa Karups. Her remarkable natural talent took her to the Royal Academy of Music in Stockholm, where she was a student (1941–46) of the renowned tenor Joseph Hislop. Though Nilsson had made her operatic debut at Stockholm's Royal Theater in 1944, her debut in leading roles came with the Stockholm company two years later, as Agathe in Carl Weber's *Der Freischütz*. Her first great success followed in 1947 as Lady Macbeth in Verdi's *Macbeth*. For the next five years, she sang throughout Europe and created a sensation in England at the 1951 Glyndebourne Festival as Elettra in Mozart's *Idomeneo*. At the same time, in a transformation much like that of the Wagnerian soprano Kirsten Flagstad a generation earlier, Nilsson's voice was maturing and changing in ways that made it more brilliant, powerful, and dramatic. With an unusual precision in attacking a note and a keen sense of pitch, her voice could slice through the heaviest orchestral textures, and it had the sheer power and clarion edge to ride over the sound of the orchestra without the slightest appearance of strain. In 1954, she began singing the great soprano roles in Richard Wagner's music-dramas, making a particularly strong impression as Brünnhilde in *Götterdämmerung* that season in Stockholm, Vienna, Munich, and at the Wagner festival in Bayreuth. Nilsson

BIRGIT NILSSON AS AIDA.

49 ♪

was immediately hailed as Flagstad's successor in the Wagner repertoire, and she enjoyed a succession of triumphant debuts in Europe and the United States throughout the 1950s. She was a regular visitor at the Bayreuth Festival from 1959 until 1970, and sang Brünnhilde in the first complete stereo recording of Wagner's *Der Ring des Nibelungen* cycle. As she was being acclaimed as a

Wagnerian, Nilsson made a point of continuing to sing Italian roles, particularly a selection of Verdi heroines and the title roles in Puccini's *Turandot* and *Tosca.* Aida was a role she sang onstage with great success through the 1960s. She was also acclaimed in the title roles of Richard Strauss's *Salome* and *Elektra,* and, late in her career, began singing the role of the Dyer's Wife in Strauss's *Die Frau ohne Schatten.* The quality of

BIRGIT NILSSON (AIDA) WITH MARIO SERENI (AMONASRO) IN ACT II.

Nilsson's singing seemed to defy age and the passage of time, and her long career ended in 1982 with her voice virtually undiminished in its power and brilliance. A beloved figure in the world of opera, she became a busy teacher of master classes after she retired. In the spring of 1996, after making a charming speech about conductor James Levine at a Metropolitan Opera gala in his honor, Nilsson astonished the audience by greeting Levine with a few bars of Brünnhilde's soaring war cry from *Die Walküre*—her voice still pristine and invincible at the age of seventy-seven.

FRANCO CORELLI (Radamès) was the most charismatic Italian tenor of his generation—tall and handsome, possessed with a powerful and incandescent voice, he was a performer who delivered onstage and in the recording studio with an almost ferocious intensity. Born in 1921 in Ancona, Italy, Corelli trained as a naval architect before entering the Pesaro Conservatory to study voice in 1947. He soon quit the conservatory, losing patience with academic training, and taught himself operatic roles by listening to recordings of the great singers. Whatever hurdles it may have created for him, Corelli's unorthodox development resulted in an extraordinary singing style that was evident in his professional debut at the Spoleto Festival in 1952 as Don José in *Carmen*. The sound of Corelli's voice was fundamentally arresting in its propulsive brilliance and expressive range. He sang with a beautiful sense of line that impressed with its poetry. But it was intensity that defined his style, and his passion as a performer seemed, to some observers, to verge on hysteria. His high notes, over which he fretted and worried his whole career, were miraculous both in their vibrant, full-bodied power and in his ability to control them (listen, on this recording, to the diminuendo he executes on the high B-flat at the end of the aria "Celeste

Aida"). Corelli made his debut at La Scala, Milan, in 1954, after a brief stint with provincial Italian companies, and became a star there as well as at the Maggio Musicale Fiorentino (Florence May Festival) and in open-air performances at the Arena di Verona. Highlights of Corelli's repertoire included, in addition to Don José, Canio in *I pagliacci,* Turiddu in *Cavalleria rusticana,* Radamès in *Aida,* Don Alvaro in *La forza del destino,* Manrico in *Il trovatore,* Pollione in *Norma,* Cavaradossi in *Tosca,* Roméo in Gounod's *Roméo et Juliette,* and Calaf in *Turandot,* as well as the title roles in *Andrea Chénier, Ernani,* and *Werther.* International debuts throughout the 1950s—at the Vienna Staatsoper, the Paris Opéra, London's Covent Garden, and in San Francisco and Chicago—established him as the world's most exciting tenor in a generation that included Mario del Monaco, Richard Tucker, and Giuseppe di Stefano. Corelli made his Metropolitan Opera debut in *Il trovatore* on the same legendary night as Leontyne Price. Though some critics derided Corelli for the unabashed intensity of his performances, he was a brilliant exponent of a dramatic Italian vocal style that very nearly disappeared after his retirement in the early 1970s. He never masked how difficult psychologically and emotionally he found the process of performing, which may be the reason he retired from singing while his voice was still in excellent condition. Despite the vogue for more lyrical tenor singing that came with the popularity of Luciano Pavarotti and Plácido Domingo, Corelli has re-emerged through recordings and videos as one of the most admired tenors of the century.

FRANCO CORELLI AS RADAMÈS.

GRACE BUMBRY (Amneris) has had a remarkable career as a mezzo-soprano, with occasional forays into the soprano repertory. Born in 1937 in St. Louis, she began singing in church choirs as a little girl and arrived at Northwestern University in 1955, where she was a student of Lotte Lehmann. Bumbry followed Lehmann to the Music Academy of the West in Santa Barbara, California, to continue the study that would shape her as a singer. Her professional debut came in a concert performance in London in 1959 and her operatic debut, a year later, where she stunned audiences at the Paris Opéra as a last-minute substitute in the role of Amneris in *Aida*. The fact that she was African American added to the glamour of the debut, and it created a positive furor when Wieland Wagner subsequently signed her to sing the role of Venus in Wagner's *Tannhäuser* at the 1961 Bayreuth Festival. The triumph Bumbry enjoyed there made her an instant celebrity. Her return to the United States brought her to the Kennedy White House and, subsequently, she embarked on an important concert tour. Her debut at the Chicago Lyric Opera in 1963 repeated her Bayreuth success as Venus, and she made her Metropolitan Opera debut two years later as Princess Eboli in Verdi's *Don Carlo*. Bumbry's Carmen created a sensation at the 1966 Salzburg Festival under Herbert von Karajan (a production that was filmed), and it became one of her trademark roles. In the early 1970s, Bumbry took advantage of her remarkable range and began singing soprano roles. The title role in Strauss's *Salome* became a particular favorite, as did the fearsome role of Abigaille in Verdi's *Nabucco,* and she had great success in the title roles of *Tosca* and *Aida* as well. (She continued to sing the mezzo-soprano role of Amneris even as she began to sing Elisabeth as well as Venus in *Tannhäuser*.) Bumbry also sang Bess

GRACE BUMBRY AS AMNERIS.

in the first Metropolitan Opera production of Gershwin's *Porgy and Bess*. In the 1980s, she returned to the great mezzo-soprano roles upon which her reputation rested. Her voice was remarkable for its expressive richness, power, and extensive range—qualities largely undiminished when she returned to the Metropolitan Opera for a gala appearance in 1996.

MARIO SERENI (Amonasro) enjoyed great popularity in the 1950s and 1960s in the important baritone roles of the Italian repertoire, both in major international houses and on recordings. Born in Perugia, Italy, in 1928, Sereni attended Rome's Accademia de Santa Cecilia and the Accademia Chigiana in Siena, where he was the student of Mario Basiola. His professional career began on an unusually high level in 1953—at the Maggio Musicale Fiorentino (Florence May Festival)—and within four years, he had made his Metropolitan Opera debut as Carlo Gérard in *Andrea Chénier* and had also sung at Buenos Aires's Teatro Colón. Sereni enjoyed a long and steady career at the Metropolitan Opera, London's Covent Garden, Milan's La Scala, the Vienna Staatsoper, and other companies around the world. Despite his success, however, Sereni remained in the shadow of the more charismatic baritones of his time—principally Leonard Warren, Tito Gobbi, Robert Merrill, Ettore Bastianini, Piero Cappuccilli, and Rolando Panerai—and critics frequently dismissed his singing. Yet his many recordings (he can be heard on the legendary *Lisbon Traviata* recording of 1958 with Maria Callas and Alfredo Kraus) reveal a singer and musician of considerable distinction, with a handsome voice, a durable technique, and a fine sense of style.

MARIO SERENI AS AMONASRO.

ZUBIN MEHTA is a leading figure in the generation of "superstar" conductors that appeared on the scene in the early 1960s. Mehta was born in Bombay in 1936, the son of the Indian violinist and conductor Mehli Mehta, who was descended from a Zoroastrian tribe of Parsi noblemen that had emigrated to India from Persia hundreds of years earlier. His first teacher was his father, who also founded the Bombay Symphony Orchestra and served as its concertmaster and later as its conductor. Mehta was only sixteen when he conducted a rehearsal of that orchestra. Though he briefly toyed with the idea of a career in medicine, his eventual decision to become a musician led him to Vienna, where he played double bass and studied conducting at the Academy of Music with Hans Swarowsky. After further study in Siena with Carlo Zecchi and Alceo Galliera, Mehta graduated from the Vienna Academy of Music in 1957, and the following year he won a conducting competition sponsored by the Royal Liverpool Philharmonic Orchestra. Successful guest appearances in Europe and the United States led to his appointment in 1960 as musical director of the Montreal Symphony Orchestra. Two years later, he was named musical director of the Los Angeles Philharmonic Orchestra, and for five years he held both posts, one of the first conductors to take full advantage of jet travel in order to sustain such a schedule. Mehta remained in Los Angeles, where he was enormously popular, until he was named Pierre Boulez's successor at the New York Philharmonic in 1978. Though he remained in New York longer than any musical director in that orchestra's history, Mehta was not as warmly appreciated there as he was in Los Angeles. He is more closely identified with the Israel

ZUBIN MEHTA BEFORE THE ANCIENT ISRAELI FORTRESS OF MASADA.

Philharmonic, to which he was named music adviser in 1968 and musical director in 1977. His connection with Israel runs deep—he conducted the Israel Philharmonic in dramatic, morale-building concerts during the Six-Day War in 1967 and on Mount Scopus for the twenty-fifth anniversary of Israel's independence. Throughout his career, Mehta has been a highly respected opera conductor, though his opera appearances in the United States have been comparatively rare. It was with *Aida* that he made his Metropolitan Opera debut in 1965. He has conducted opera in all of the major European houses and in numerous recordings, and has been seen by hundreds of millions as the conductor of the blockbuster Three Tenors concerts of 1990 and 1994. Mehta's exuberant, larger-than-life personality makes him a compelling figure on the podium, and the aura of celebrity he generates has led some critics to dismiss him as more of a showman than a serious musician. Yet for all of his glamour, his abilities as a conductor are remarkable, and his technical command astonishing and comprehensive, particularly in the realm of opera and in the late Romantic and early twentieth-century repertoire.

EMI RECORDING SESSION OF
AIDA: LEFT TO RIGHT: BIRGIT
NILSSON, MARIO SERENI,
THE REPETITEUR, FRANCO
CORELLI (HIDDEN), BONALDO
GIAIOTTI, AND GRACE BUMBRY.

The

Libretto

Act 1

FROM ACT I OF A SAN DIEGO OPERA PRODUCTION.

Prelude The theme that identifies Aida is heard immediately and disarmingly in the strings; it is a melody at once beautiful and sad. It evolves swiftly throughout the orchestra, answered by the heavy tread of a melody **(01:13)** that will be associated with the all-powerful Egyptian priests. The two melodies are ingeniously brought into conflict **(01:42)**—a snapshot of the drama that will follow, playing Aida's pride and passion against the formidable strength of Egyptian forces—before the clash **(01:56)** fades away, and, with tantalizing effect, Aida's melody returns **(02:01)** and effervesces in the whisper of the divided first violins.

Scene One

PRELUDE

A hall in the royal palace at Memphis.

Left and right, a colonnade decorated with statues and flowering shrubs. Rear, a great door beyond which can be seen temples, the palaces of Memphis, and the pyramids.

RAMFIS
Si, corre voce che l'Etiope ardisca
Sfidarci ancora, e del Nilo la valle
E Tebe minacciar. Fra breve un messo
Recherà il ver.

RADAMÈS
La sacra
Iside consultasti?

RAMFIS
Ella ha nomato
Dell egizie falangi
Il condottier supremo.

RAMFIS
Yes, it is rumoured that the Ethiopian has dared to challenge us again, threatening Thebes and the valley of the Nile. Shortly a messenger will bring us the details.

RADAMÈS
Have you consulted
Holy Isis?

RAMFIS
She has named
the supreme commander
of the Egyptian armies.

RADAMÈS
Oh, lui felice!

RAMFIS *(con intenzione, fissando Radamès)*
Giovane e prode è desso.
Ora del nume
Reco i decreti al Re.

RADAMÈS
Oh, fortunate man!

RAMFIS *(looking steadily at Radamès, meaningfully)*
He is young and brave. Now I shall go to inform the King of the deity's decree.

Ramfis goes out.

THE LEGENDARY ENRICO CARUSO AS RADAMÈS, C. 1908.

disc no. 1/track 3 *Se quel guerriero io fossi!* Fanfares underscore Radamès's excitement about the coming war and his hope that he will be the leader the Egyptian army. But when his thoughts turn to Aida **(00:33)**, the music melts for a moment. His ambition then overrides his emotions **(00:42)** until a final fanfare dies away, leaving muted violins **(00:58)** that lure him into a dream of his beloved.

LUCIANO
PAVAROTTI
SINGING
"CELESTE
AIDA."

disc no. 1/track 4 *Celeste Aida* Radamès's first aria comes cruelly early in the opera, leaving the tenor little time to warm up. It is a strikingly Verdian aria, calling for great tenderness while insisting on a powerful and heroic sound. Its rising arcs of melody beautifully phrase Radamès's radiant images of Aida and his adoration of her. The tenor must sing two B-flats in this aria, and the second is marked *pianissimo morendo,* suggesting a soft, quietly ecstatic sound. Few tenors can achieve the effect, and even fewer try. (Verdi apparently accepted this as inevitable, and even approved an alternative ending.) In this recording, Franco Corelli does it **(03:18)**, scaling back the final B-flat to a rapt pianissimo.

RADAMÈS *(solo)*
Se quel guerriero
Io fossi! Se il mio sogno
Se avverasse! Un esercito di prodi
Da me guidato, e la vittoria e il plauso
Di Menfi tutta! E a te, mia dolce Aida,
Tonar di lauri cinto...
Dirti: per te ho pugnato, per te ho vinto!
Celeste Aida, forma divina.
Mistico serto di luce e fior,
Del mio pensiero tu sei regina,
Tu di mia vita sei lo splendor.
Il tuo bel cielo vorrei ridarti,
Le dolci brezze del patrio suol,
Un regal serto cul crin posarti,
Ergerti un trono vicino al sol.
Oh! Celeste Aida, forma divina,
Mistico raggio di luce e fior,
Del mio pensiero *ecc.*

RADAMÈS *(solo)*
If only that warrior were I!
If my dream might come true!
An army of brave men, led by me—
victory, and the applause of all Memphis!
To return to you, my sweet Aida,
decked with the victor's laurels,
to say, "I fought, I won for you!"
Heavenly Aida, divine form,
mystic garland of light and flowers,
you are the queen of my thought,
you are the splendour of my life.
That I might bring you once more
the blue skies, the soft breezes of your
native land, a royal crown to deck your
brow, a royal throne for you, in the sun!
Oh, heavenly Aida, divine form,
mystic halo of light and flowers,
you are the queen, *etc.*

Amneris enters.

AMNERIS

Quale insolita gioia
Nel tuo sguardo! Di quale
Nobil fierezza ti balena il volto!
Degna di invidia, oh! quanto
Saria la donna il cui bramato aspetto
Tanta luce di gaudio in te destasse!

RADAMÈS

D'un sogno avventuroso
Si beava il mio cuore. Oggi, la Diva
Profferse il nome deal guerrier che al
campo
Le schiere egzie condurrà. O, s'io fossi
A tale onor prescelto...

AMNERIS

Né un altro sogno mai
Più gentil, più soave
Al core ti parlò? Non hai tu in Menfi
Desideri, speranze?

RADAMÈS

Io! (Quale inchiesta!
Forse l'arcano amore
Scopri che m'arde in core...
Della sua schiava il nome
Mi lesse nel pensier!)

AMNERIS

(Oh! guai se un altro amore
Ardesse a lui nel core!
Guai se il mio sguardo penetra
Questo fatal mister!)

AMNERIS

What rare joy shines
on your face! What noble pride
flashes in your eyes!
How enviable indeed
would be that woman whose beloved face
might kindle so joyful a light in you!

RADAMÈS

My heart was lost
in an adventurous dream. Today the goddess has named the warrior who will lead
the Egyptian legions into battle.
Ah! If I were
chosen for such an honour...

AMNERIS

Was it not perhaps
some greater, sweeter dream
which spoke to you heart? Have you
no desires, no hopes, here in Memphis?

RADAMÈS

I! (What an interrogation!
Perhaps she has discovered
the secret love which burns in my heart...
perhaps she has read in my thoughts
her slave girl's name!)

AMNERIS

(Oh, woe if love for another
should burn in his heart!
Woe to him if my eyes
should see through this fatal mystery!)

RADAMÈS *(vedendo Aida)*
Dessa!

AMNERIS *(da sè, osservando)*
Ei si turba, e quale
Sguardo rivolse a lei!
Aida! A me rivale
Forse saria costei?

She turns to Aida.

RADAMÈS *(seeing Aida)*
It is she!

AMNERIS *(to herself)*
He is moved! The glance
with which he looked at her!
Aida! Could it be she
who is my rival?

---

disc no. 1/track 6 — *Vieni, o diletta, appressati* Heralded by her theme **(02:35, track 5)**, Aida arrives in the middle of a confrontation between Radamès and Amneris. In a trio that reflects Verdi's genius for weaving the complex strands of a human drama in clearly defined musical terms, the jealous Amneris discerns the truth about the furtive lovers. The tension is palpable **(01:27)**: each of them suffers a different kind of pain. Verdi's scoring is masterful, right down to the pulsing of the tympani **(01:50)** under the quiet desperation of the trio, suggesting the wild beating of the human heart.

Vieni, o diletta, appressati,
Schiava non sei né ancella
Qui dove in dolce fascino
Io ti chiamai sorella.
Piangi? Delle tue lacrime
Svela il segreto a me.

AIDA
Ohimè! di guerra fremere
L'atroce grido io sento,
Per l'infelice patria,
Per me, per voi pavento.

Come, my child, come near me.
You are neither slave nor handmaiden
here, where for love of you
I have called you sister. You weep?
Tell me the reason for your tears,
tell me your secret.

AIDA
Alas, I have heard
the frightful war-cry sound,
I fear for my country,
for myself, for you.

AMNERIS
Favelli il ver? né s'agita
Più grave cura in te?

aside, looking at Aida

Trema, o rea schiava, ah! trema
Ch'io nel tuo cor discenda!
Trema che il ver m'apprenda
Quel pianto e quel rossor!

RADAMÈS *(fra sè, guardando Amneris)*
Nel volto a lei balena
Lo sdegno ed il sospetto.
Guai se l'arcano affetto
A noi leggesse il cor!

AIDA *(fra sè)*
No, sull'afflitta patria
Non geme il cor soltanto;
Quello ch'io verso è pianto
Di sventurato amor.

The King enters, preceded by his guard and followed by Ramfis, ministers, priests, officers, and others.

IL RE
Alta cagion v'aduna,
O fidi Egizi, al vostro Re d'intorno.
Dai confin d'Etiopia un messaggero
Dianzi giungea; gravi novelle ei reca.
Vi piaccia udirlo.

to an officer

AMNERIS
Is this true? No greater care
disturbs you?

Ah! Tremble, evil slave, tremble!
Let me sound your heart!
Tremble, for the truth is clear to me
when I see your tears, your blushes!

RADAMÈS *(aside, looking at Amneris)*
In her face, anger
and suspicion blaze like a fire.
Woe if our secret love
she should ever read in our hearts!

AIDA *(to herself)*
No, not only for my country
is my heart in anguish;
the tears I shed are the tears of my
unhappy love!

THE KING
High reasons of state have led me
to summon you, O faithful Egyptians.
A messenger has arrived
from Ethiopia. He brings grave tidings.
Hear them now.

Il messagger s'avanzi!

The messenger enters.

MESSAGGERO
Il sacro suolo dell'Egitto è invaso
Dai barbari Etiopi;
I nostri campi
Fur devastati, arse le messi, e baldi
Della facil vittoria i predatori
Già marciano su Tebe!

TUTTI
Ed osan tanto!

MESSAGGERO
Un guerriero indomabile, feroce,
Li conduce: Amonasro.

TUTTI
Il Re!

AIDA *(a parte)*
Mio padre!

MESSAGGERO
Già Tebe è in armi e dalle cento porte
Sul barbaro invasore
Prorompèrà, guerra recando e morte.

IL RE
Sì: guerra e morte
il nostro grido sia!

Let the messenger come forward.

MESSENGER
The sacred soil of Egypt has been invaded
by the fierce Ethiopian.
Our fields have been laid waste,
our crops burned.
Spurred on by this easy victory, the foe
is marching now on Thebes.

ALL
They dare to do this!

MESSENGER
A fierce, relentless warrior leads them—
Amonasro!

ALL
The King himself!

AIDA *(to herself)*
My father!

MESSENGER
Thebes, already in arms, will fall
upon the barbarian invader from her
hundred gates, spreading war and death.

THE KING
Yes! Let war and death
be our battle cry!

TUTTI
Guerra! Guerra! *ecc.*
Tremenda, inesorata!

IL RE *(accostandosi a Radamès)*
Iside venerata
Di nostre schiere invitte
Già designava il condottier supremo:
Radamès.

TUTTI
Radamès!

RADAMÈS
Ah! sien grazie ai numi!
Son paghi voti miei!

AMNERIS *(fra sè)*
Ei duce!

AIDA *(fra sè)*
Io tremo!

MINISTRI E CAPITANI
Radamès! Radamès!

IL RE
Or di Vulcano al tempio
Muovi, o guerrier. Le sacre
Armi ti cingi e alla vittoria vola.
Su! del Nilo al sacro lido
Accorrete, egizi eroi;
Da ogni cor prorompa il grido
Guerra e morte allo stranier!

ALL
War! War! *etc.*
Tremendous, pitiless war!

THE KING *(coming near to Radamès)*
Holy Isis
has already named the leader
of our invincible legions:
Radamès!

ALL
Radamès!

RADAMÈS
Ah! praised be the gods!
My prayers are answered!

AMNERIS *(to herself)*
He, the leader!

AIDA *(to herself)*
I am afraid!

MINISTERS AND CAPTAINS
Radamès! Radamès!

THE KING
Go now, O warrior,
to the Temple of Vulcan. There put on
the sacred arms; go forth to victory!
Onward! Go forth, Egyptian heroes,
to the sacred banks of the Nile.
From every heart let the cry sound out—
War and death to the invader!

THE TRIUMPHAL SCENE
FROM A 1940 PRODUCTION
AT THE METROPOLITAN OPERA.

RAMFIS
Gloria ai numi! ognun rammenti
Ch'essi direggono gli eventi,
Che in poter dei numi solo
Stan le sorti del guerrier.
Ognun rammenti. Che in poter, *ecc.*

RAMFIS
Glory to the gods! Let all remember,
it is they who rule our destinies.
Only the power of the gods
can dictate the warrior's fate.
Let all remember that only the power, *etc.*

disc no. 1/track 8 *Su! del Nilo al sacro lido* With the news of the Ethiopian invasion, the passion for war finally erupts in this pompous march led by the king. It shudders forward inexorably, with everyone joining in **(00:40)**, even Aida, who despairs of her torn sympathies **(00:58)**. As the ensemble grows to an almost hysterical pitch **(01:37)**, Amneris shouts farewell to Radamès with the words "Ritorna vincitor" **(02:20)**, which the crowd echoes as it jubilantly marches away.

MINISTRI E CAPITANI
Su! del Nilo al sacro lido
Sien barriera i nostri petti;
Non echeggi che un sol grido
Guerra e morte allo stranier! *ecc.*

MINISTERS AND CAPTAINS
Onward! May our breasts be a fortress
shielding the sacred banks of the Nile.
Let no cry sound but our united cry,
War, war, and death to the invader! *etc.*

IL RE
Su! del Nilo, *ecc.*

THE KING
Go forth, Egyptian heroes, *etc.*

AIDA *(fra sè)*
Per chi piango? per chi prego?
Qual potere m'avvince a lui!
Deggio amarlo ed è costui
Un nemico uno stranier!

AIDA *(to herself)*
For whom do I weep? For whom do I pray?
What power binds me to him?
I must love him, yet he is
the enemy of my country!

RADAMÈS

Sacro fremito di gloria
Tutta l'anima m'investe.
Su! corriamo alla vittoria!
Guerra e morte allo stranier!

AMNERIS *(recando una bandiera e consegnandola a Radamès)*

Di mia man ricevi, o duce,
Il vessillo glorioso;
Ti sia guida, ti sia luce
Della gloria sul sentier.

IL RE

Su! del Nilo al sacro lido, *ecc.*

RAMFIS, SACERDOTI

Gloria ai Numi, *ecc.*

MINISTRI E CAPITANI

Su! del Nilo, *ecc.*

RADAMÈS, MESSAGGERO

Su! Corriamo alle vittoria, *ecc.*

AMNERIS

Tis sia guida, *ecc.*

TUTTI

Guerra! guerra! *ecc.*
Sterminio all'invasor! *ecc.*

RADAMÈS

A sacred thrill of glory
runs through my heart.
Onward, let us hasten to victory!
War and death to the invader!

AMNERIS *(bearing a banner, which she presents to Radamès)*

Accept, O leader, from my hands
this glorious banner;
may it be as a light and a guide on the road to victory.

THE KING

Onward, Egyptian heroes, *etc.*

RAMFIS AND PRIESTS

Glory to the Gods, *etc.*

MINISTERS AND CAPTAINS

Onward! May our breasts, *etc.*

RADAMÈS AND MESSENGER

Onward, let us hasten to victory, *etc.*

AMNERIS

May it be as a light, *etc.*

ALL

War! War! *etc.*
Death to the invader, *etc.*

disc no. 1/track 9 *Ritorna vincitor!* Suddenly left alone, Aida echoes the words "ritorna vincitor," shocked that she could have uttered them. In a mighty recitative section, she dramatically contemplates what she has wished on her homeland. She finally breaks down; her frustration over her difficult situation is reflected in a breathless melody **(03:06)**. Its momentum abates only when Aida seems to retreat into a childlike state **(03:50)**, crooning pitiably to the gods for deliverance from her anguish.

LEONTYNE
PRICE AS
AIDA.

AMNERIS
Ritorna vincitor!

TUTTI
Ritorna vincitor!

They all leave, except Aida.

AIDA
Ritorna vincitor! E dal mio labbro
Uscì l'empia parola! Vincitor
Del padre mio di lui che impugna l'armi
Per me per ridarmi
Una patria, una reggia e il nome illustre
Che qui celar m'è forza. Vincitor
De' miei fratelli...ond'io lo vegga, tinto
Del sangue amato, trionfar nel plauso
Dell'egizie coorti! E dietro il carro,
Un Re, mio padre, di catene avvinto!
L'insana parola,
O numi, sperdete!
Al seno d'un padre
La figlia rendete;
Struggete le squadre
Dei nostri oppressor!
Ah! Sventurata! che dissi? E'lamor mio?
Dunque scordar poss'io
Questo fervido amore che oppressa
e schiava
Come raio di sol qui mi beava?
Imprecherò la morte
A Radamès, a lui ch'amo pur tanto!
Ah! non fu in terra mai
Da più crudeli angosce un core affranto!

AMNERIS
Return victorious!

ALL
Return victorious!

AIDA
Return victorious! My lips have spoken
the traitorous words! Victorious
over my father, who takes up arms
for me, to give me again
a country, a kingdom, and a great name,
which here I must hide. Victorious
over my brothers—that I may see him,
stained with the beloved blood, welcomed
in triumph by Egypt! And behind
his chariot, a king, my father, in chains!
My mad word,
O gods, efface!
Send back this child
to her father's heart.
Destroy the legions
of our oppressors!
Wretched girl, what have I said? And my
love?
Can I, then, forget
this burning love, which, as a wretched
slave,
I welcomed in rapture like a ray of the sun?
Shall I invoke death
upon Radamès, him whom I love so much?
Ah, never on earth

I sacri nomi di padre, d'amante
Nè profferir poss'io, ne ricordar;
Per l'un, per l'altro confusa e tremante.
Io piangere vorrei, vorrei pregar.
Ma la mia prece in bestemmia si muta...
Delitto è il pianto a me, colpa il sospir...
In notte cupa la mente è perduta,
E nell'ansia crudel vorrei morir.
Numi, pietà del mio soffrir!
Speme non v'ha pel mio dolor.
Amor fatal, tremendo amor,
Spezzami il cor, fammi morir!
Numi, pietà del mio soffrir! ecc.

has a broken heart known such anguish!
The sacred words *father* and *lover*—
I can no longer speak them, nor remember.
For each, in my fear and confusion,
I should like to pray, to weep.
But my prayer changes to cursing—
tears, for me, are criminal; so too my sighs.
My mind is lost in a bitter night,
and in such cruel anguish I wish to die.
Oh! gods, have pity on my suffering!
There is no hope for my sorrow!
Fatal love, fearful love,
break my heart and let me die!
Oh! gods, have pity on my suffering! etc.

Scene Two   Interior of the temple of Vulcan at Memphis.

A mysterious light shines down from above. There is a low row of columns
that disappears into the distance. Statues of various gods. At mid-scene, on a
scaffolding covered with tapestries, stands the altar decorated with sacred
symbols. The smoke of incense rises from censers hanging on golden tripods.
Priests and priestesses. Ramfis is at the foot of the altar.

SACERDOTESSA
Possente Fthà, del mondo
Spirito animator, ah!

PRIESTESS
Mighty, mighty Phtha, life-giving
spirit of the world, ah!

COL CORO DELLE SACERDOTESSE
Noi t'invochiamo!

WITH CHORUS OF PRIESTESSES
We invoke thee!

RAMFIS E SACERDOTI
Tu che dal nulla hai tratto L'onde,

RAMFIS AND PRIESTS
Thou, who from nothingness didst draw

la terra, il ciel,
Noi t'invochiam!

SACERDOTESSA
Immenso Fthà, del mondo
Spirito fecondator, ah!

COL CORO DELLE SACERDOTESSE
Noi t'invochiamo!

RAMFIS E SACERDOTI
Nume, che del tuo spirito
Sei figlio e genitor,
Noi t'invochiam!

SACERDOTESSA
Fuoco increato, eterno,
Onde ebbe luce il sol, ah!

COL CORO DELLE SACERDOTESSE
Noi t'invichiamo!

RAMFIS E SACERDOTI
Via dell'universo,
Mito d'eterno amor,
Noi t'invochiam!

the seas, the earth, the heavens,
we invoke thee!

PRIESTESS
Great, great Phtha, fruitful spirits of the
world, ah!

WITH CHORUS OF PRIESTESSES
We invoke thee!

RAMFIS AND PRIESTS
God, who art of thy spirit
both son and father,
we invoke thee!

PRIESTESS
Uncreated, eternal flame,
which sparked the sun, ah!

WITH CHORUS OF PRIESTESSES
We invoke thee!

RAMFIS AND PRIESTS
Life of the Universe,
mythus of eternal love,
we invoke thee!

Radamès is brought into the temple. He carries no weapons. As he goes to the altar, the priestesses perform the sacred dance. The priests, meanwhile, place a silver veil over Radamès's head.

Sacred dance of the Priestesses.

SACERDOTESSE
Immenso Fthà!

PRIESTESSES
Great Phtha!

RAMFIS E SACERDOTI
Noi t'invochiam!

RAMFIS AND PRIESTS
We invoke thee!

RAMFIS (*a Radamès*)
Mortal, diletto ai numi,
A te fidate son e'Egitto le sorti.
Il sacro brando
Dal dio temprato,
Per tua man diventi
A nemici terror, folgore, morte.

RAMFIS (*to Radamès*)
O youth, beloved of the gods,
you hold in trust the destiny of Egypt.
May the sacred sword,
tempered by the gods,
become in your hand
blazing terror and death for the enemy.

SACERDOTI
Il sacro brando, *ecc.*

PRIESTS
May the sacred sword, *etc.*

RAMFIS (*volgendosi al nume*)
Nume, custode e vindice
Di questa sacra terra,
La mano tua distendi
Sovra l'egizio suol.

RAMFIS (*to the god*)
O god, custodian and avenger
of this sacred land,
lift thy hand
over the land of Egypt.

RADAMÈS
Nume, che duce ed arbitro
Sei d'ogni umana guerra,
Proteggi tu, difendi
D'Egitto il sacro suol, *ecc.*

RADAMÈS
O god, leader and judge
of every earthly battle,
protect thou, defend thou
the sacred soil of Egypt! *etc.*

disc no. 1/track 12 *Nume, custode e vindice* After the priests beseech the god Phtha for his assistance and Radamès is brought in, Ramfis sings a solemn prayer for Egypt's deliverance **(00:14)**—an engrossing, minor-key melody typical of Verdi's solution of effectively suggesting a musical style for ancient Egypt. It is punctuated by echoes of the High Priestess's hymn to Phtha **(01:50)** and, as a benediction, the entire awed assemblage in the temple shouts the words "Immenso Phtha!".

RAMFIS, SACERDOTI
La mano tua distendi
Sovra l'egizio suol.
Nume, custode e vindice, *ecc.*

RAMFIS AND PRIESTS
Lift thy hand
over the land of Egypt.
O god, custodian and avenger, *etc.*

While Radamès is being invested with the sacred arms, the priests and priestesses resume the sacred hymn and the mystic dance.

TUTTI
Possente Fthà, del mondo, *ecc.*

ALL
Mighty Phtha, creator of the world, *etc.*

Act Two

Scene One   *A room in the apartments of Amneris.*

Amneris is surrounded by slave girls who are dressing for the victory celebration. Incense is burning in censers hanging from tripods. Youthful Moorish slaves dance about her as they wave great feather fans.

SCHIAVE
Chi mai fra gl'inni e i plausi
Erge alla gloria il vol,
Al par d'un dio terribile,
Fulgente al par del sol,
Vieni: sul crin ti piovano
Contesti ai lauri i fior;
Suonin di gloria i cantici
Coi cantici d'amor.

AMNERIS *(fra sè)*
Ah, vieni, amor mio, m'inebria...
Fammi beato il cor!

SCHIAVE
Or dove son le barbare
Orde dello stranier?
Siccome nebbia sparvero
Al soffio del guerrier.
Vieni: di gloria il premio
Raccogli, o vincitor,

SLAVE GIRLS
O hero, who, to the sounds of hymns and
praise, set forth on the flight to glory,
like some god of terror,
blazing like the sun,
come, on our head shall shower
the blossoms won from the laurel,
and together the songs of glory
shall sound with the songs of love.

AMNERIS *(to herself)*
Ah, come, my love, bring madness
and blessed peace to my heart!

SLAVE GIRLS
Now where are the barbaric hordes
of the mighty invader?
Like mist, they faded away
at the first breath of our champion.
Come, victorious warrior,
come take the prize of glory;

T'arrise la vittoria,	victory has smiled upon you,
T'arriderà l'amor.	on you love too shall smile.

AMNERIS *(fra sè)*
Ah, vieni, amor mio, ravvivami
D'un caro accento ancor!

AMNERIS *(to herself)*
Ah, come, my love, give new life to me,
once more, with words of love!

Dance of the Moorish slaves.

disc no. 1/track 15 *Vieni, sul crin ti piovano* Here begins the great duet of Aida and Amneris. It is not a duet in the traditional sense, but it is one of opera's most formidable confrontations—a mesmerizing cat-and-mouse game played out with fascinating complexity in less than fifteen minutes of music and action **(running through track 18)**. Verdi's orchestra brilliantly reflects Amneris's considerable and deftly wielded cruelty, as well as Aida's ever-increasing despair. The scene ends with the fanfares of the Triumphal Scene gathering in the distance and Aida once again begging the gods for peace.

SCHIAVE
Vieni sul crin ti piovano, *ecc.*

SLAVE GIRLS
Come, on your head, shall shower, *etc.*

AMNERIS
Ah, vieni, amor mio, m'inebria, *ecc.*
Silenzio! Aida verso noi s'avanza...
Figlia de'vinti, il suo dolor m'è sacro.

AMNERIS
Ah, come, my love, *etc.*
Silence! Aida is coming.
Child of the vanquished, her grief is sacred.

At a sign from Amneris, all withdraw.

Nel rivederla, il dubbio
Atroce in me si desta . . .
Il mistero fatal si squarci alfine!

Seeing her now, the fearful
doubt awakens in me again—
now I shall penetrate this fatal secret!

AMNERIS
(GRACE
BUMBRY),
RIGHT, AND
AIDA (MARTINA
ARROYO).

to Aida, with feigned tenderness

Fu la sorte dell'armi a'tuoi funesta,
Povera Aida! Il lutto
Che ti pesa sul cor teco divido.
Io son l'amica tua...
Tutto da me tu avrai, vivrai felice!

the fortunes of war have gone against
your people! Poor Aida!
Your heart's grief I share with you.
I am your friend. You shall have
whatever you wish from me. You shall be
happy.

AIDA

Felice esser poss'io
Lungi dal suol natio...
Qui dove ignota
M'è la sorte del padre e dei fratelli?

AIDA

Can I be happy,
far from my homeland,
knowing nothing of the fate
of my father and my brothers?

AMNERIS

Ben ti compiango! pure hanno un confine
I mali di quaggiù. Sanerà il tempo
Le angosce del tuo core,
E più che il tempo, un dio possente...
Amore.

AMNERIS

I weep for you. But there are limits
to earthly sorrow. Time will quiet
the anguish of your heart—
and, more than time, a powerful god—
Love!

AIDA *(vivamente commossa)*

Amore, amore! Gaudio, tormento,
Soave ebbrezza, ansia crudel!
Ne' tuoi sorriso mi schiude il ciel.
Ne' tuoi dotori, *ecc.*

AIDA *(to herself)*

Love, love! Tormenting joy, sweet rapture,
cruel anxiety! In thy sorrow I find my life,
in thy smile, I find heaven itself.
In thy sorrow, *etc.*

AMNERIS *(fra sè, guardando Aida fissamente)*

Ah! quel pallore, quel turbamento
Svelan l'arcana febbre d'amor!
D'interrogarla quasi ho sgomento,
Divido l'ansie del suo terror.

AMNERIS *(to herself)*

Ah, her pallor, her confusion
betray the secret fever of love!
I fear to question her,
for I share the anxiety of her heart!

℃88

Ebben, qual nuovo fremito
T'assal, gentile Aida?
I tuoi segreti svelami,
All'amor mio t'affida.
Tra i forti che pugnarono
Della tua patria a danno.
Qualcuno un dolce affano
Forse a te in cor destò?

AIDA
Che parli?

AMNERIS
A tutti barbara
Non si mostrò la sorte,
Se in campo il duce impavido
Cadde trafitto a morte...

AIDA
Che mai dicesti! ahi, misera!

AMNERIS
Sì. Radamès da'tuoi fu spento.

AIDA
Misera!

AMNERIS
E pianger puoi?

AIDA
Per sempre io piangerò!

What new anguish
disturbs you, sweet Aida?
Tell me your secret,
trust in my friendship.
Among those brave men who fought
and conquered your homeland,
was there perhaps one whom
you loved?

AIDA
What do you mean?

AMNERIS
Not to all
has fate been cruel,
since our fearless leader has died on the
battlefield—

AIDA
What did you say? Oh! wretched!

AMNERIS
Yes, Radamès was killed by your people.

AIDA
Alas!

AMNERIS
And can you weep?

AIDA
I shall never cease my weeping!

AMNERIS
Gli dei t'han vendicata!

AIDA
Avversi sempre mi furon i numi.

AMNERIS
Ah, trema! in cor ti lessi!...
Tu l'ami...

AIDA
Io!

AMNERIS
Non mentire!
Un detto ancora e il vero saprò.
Fissami in volto...lo t'ingannai...
Radamès vive!

AIDA
Vive!
Ah, grazie, o numi!

AMNERIS
E ancor mentir tu speri?
Sì, tu l'ami!
Mal'amo anch'io, intendi tu?
Son tua rivale, figlia de'Faraoni!

AIDA
Mia rivale! Ebben, sia pure,
Anch'io son tal...
Ah! che dissi mai?
Pietà, perdono, ah!

AMNERIS
The gods have avenged you!

AIDA
The gods have always been against me.

AMNERIS
Tremble! I have read your heart—
you love him—

AIDA
I!

AMNERIS
Do not lie!
One more word and I shall know.
Look into my eyes. I deceived you—
Radamès is alive!

AIDA
Alive!
Oh, praised be the gods!

AMNERIS
And you still hope to lie to me?
Yes, you love him!
But I too love him, do you hear?
I am your rival, I, daughter of Pharaohs!

AIDA
My rival! Then so be it,
for I too am—
Ah, what am I saying?
Have pity on me; forgive me, ah!

Pietà ti prenda del mio dolor.
È vero, io l'amo d'immenso amor.
Tu sei felice, tu sei possente,
Io vivo solo per questo amor!

AMNERIS
Trema, vil schiava!
Spezza tuo core;
Segnar tua morte può questo amore;
Del tuo destino arbitra io sono,
D'odio vendetta le furie ho in cor.

AIDA
Tu sei felice, *ecc.*

AMNERIS
Trema, vil schiava, *ecc.*

CORO *(di fuori)*
Su! del Nio al sacro lido
Sien barriera i nostri petti;
Non echeggi che un sol grido
Guerra e morte allo stranier!

AMNERIS
Alla pompa che s'appresta,
Meco, o schiava, assisterai;
Tu prostrata nella polvere,
Io sul trono accanto al Re.

AIDA
Ah! pietà! Che più mi resta?
Un deserto è la mia vita;
Vivi e regna, il tuo furore

Let pity for my sorrow move you.
It is true, I love him deeply.
You are happy, you are powerful,
in my life there is nothing but my love!

AMNERIS
Fear me now, you slave!
Let your heart break;
this love can mean your death.
I am master of your fate,
and my heart rages with hate and vengeance!

AIDA
You are happy, *etc.*

AMNERIS
Fear me, you slave, *etc.*

CHORUS *(outside)*
Onward! May our breasts be a fortress
shielding the sacred banks of the Nile!
Let no cry sound but our united cry,
war and death to the invader!

AMNERIS
In the Triumph now being made ready,
you shall take part with me, O slave!
You, prostrate in the dust,
I at the King's side, on the throne!

AIDA
Ah, have pity! What is left for me?
My life is a desert.
Live, reign—soon

Io tra breve placherò.
Quest' amore che t'irrita
Nella tomba spegnerò.

AMNERIS
Vien...mi segui...e apprederai
Se lottar tu puoi con me, *ecc.*

AIDA
Ah! Pietà, *ecc.*

AMNERIS
...Se lottar tu puoi, *ecc.*

CORO *(di fuori)*
Guerra e morte allo stranier!

Amneris exits.

AIDA
Numi, pietà del mio martir,
Speme non v'ha pel mio dolor! *ecc.*

I shall appease your anger.
This love which distresses you
will die with me, in the tomb.

AMNERIS
Come, follow me. You shall see
if you are worthy to do battle with me, *etc.*

AIDA
Ah, have pity, *etc.*

AMNERIS
...if you are worthy, *etc.*

CHORUS *(outside)*
War and death to the invader!

AIDA
O gods, take pity on my suffering!
There is no hope for my sorrow! *etc.*

Scene Two   *A gate of the city of Thebes.*

In the foreground, a group of palm trees. Right, the Temple of Ammon; left, a throne covered by a purple baldaquin. To the rear, a triumphal gate. The scene is crowded with people. The King enters, followed by ministers, priests, captains, standard-bearers, slaves bearing huge feather fans, etc. Then Amneris enters, accompanied by Aida and slave girls. The King takes his place on the throne and Amneris takes her place at his left.

disc no. 1/track 19 *Gloria all'Egitto, ad Iside* The Triumphal Scene begins with the crowd roaring its patriotic fervor, which gives way to the Triumphal March **(track 20)** and its rocketing trumpet fanfares and strutting excitement. A ballet **(track 21)** is part of the festivities, featuring the spoils of victory and more hothouse Egyptian music from Verdi that summons up the unpredictable excitement of the moment. Finally, Radamès arrives in heroic splendor **(track 22)**, bringing the parade to an end. The grateful populace sings his praises, picking up echoes of the Triumphal March as the celebration ends in a hail of fanfares.

A STILL OF THE EXUBERANT ACT II BALLET STAGED
AT LA SCALA.

POPOLO
Gloria all'Egitto, ad Iside
Che il sacro suol protegge;
Al Re che il Delta regge
Inni festosi alziam, *ecc.*

DONNE
S'intrecci il loto al lauro
Sul crin dei vincitori;
Nembo gentil di fiori
Stenda sull'armi un vel.
Danziam, fanciulle egizie,
Le mistiche carole,
Come d'intorno al sole
Danzano gli astri in ciel!

SACERDOTI
Della vittoria agli arbitri
Supremi il guardo ergete;
Grazie agli dei rendete
Nel fortunato di, *ecc.*

POPOLO
Come d'intorno al sole, *ecc.*

SACERDOTI
Grazie agli Dei, *ecc.*

POPULACE
Glory to Egypt and to Isis,
protectress of the sacred land!
To the King who rules the Delta
joyful hymns we sing! *etc.*

WOMEN
Weave the lotus and the laurel
into a crown for the victors!
Let a soft cloud of flowers
veil the steel of their arms.
Let us dance, Egyptian maidens,
the mystic dances,
as, around the sun,
the stars dance in the sky!

PRIESTS
Lift your eyes to the gods,
the arbiters of victory;
give thanks to the gods
on this happy day, *etc.*

POPULACE
As, around the sun, *etc.*

PRIESTS
Give thanks to the gods, *etc.*

*The Egyptian troops, following the trumpeters, pass in review before the
King. After them come the chariots, the ensigns, the sacred vessels, and the
statues of the gods. A band of dancing girls carries the treasure won from the
enemy. Finally Radamès enters, borne on a litter covered with a baldaquin
and carried by twelve captains.*

POPOLO
Vieni, o guerriero vindice,
Vieni a gioir con noi;
Sul passo degli eroi
I lauri, i fior versiam!
Gloria! *ecc.*

SACERDOTI
Agli arbitri supremi, *ecc.*
Grazie agli Dei, *ecc.*

IL RE *(che scende dal trono per abbracciare Radamès)*
Salvator della patria, io ti saluto.
Vieni, e mia figlia di sua man ti porga
Il serto trionfale.

Radamès bows before Amneris, who offers him the crown.

Ora, a me chiedi
Quanto più brami. Nulla a te negato
Sarà in tal dì; lo giuro
per la corona mia, pei sacri numi.

RADAMÈS
Concedi in pria che innanzi
A te sian tratti i prigionier.

The Ethiopian prisoners enter, escorted by the guards. Amonasro, dressed as an officer, comes last.

RAMFIS E SACERDOTI
Grazie agli dei, *ecc.*

POPULACE
Come, O conquering hero,
come, rejoice with us.
At the feet of our heroic warriors
we cast our flowers and laurel leaves.
Glory! *etc.*

PRIESTS
To the gods, supreme arbiters, *etc.*
Give thanks to the gods, *etc.*

THE KING *(descending from his throne to embrace Radamès)*
Saviour of the fatherland, I salute you.
Come, receive from my daughter's hand
the triumphal wreath.

Now ask of me
whatever you will. Nothing shall be
denied you on this day—I swear it
by my crown, by the sacred gods.

RADAMÈS
Before I reply, let the prisoners
be brought before you.

RAMFIS AND PRIESTS
Give thanks to the gods, *etc.*

disc no. 1/track 24 *Che veggo! Egli? Mio padre!... Anch'io pugnai... Ma tu, Re, tu signore possente* With the words "Ma tu, Re, tu signori possente" **(01:47)**, Amonasro begins the most striking ensemble piece in the opera. It is a powerful encounter, one that weaves the voices of all the principal characters around the muscular melody he sings **(02:16)** as he begs for the Egyptian king for mercy. This kind of ensemble echoes Aida's roots in the French grand opera, and represents a vastly more sophisticated and sleeker version of the climactic moments that are highlights in Meyerbeer's operas.

AIDA
Che veggo! Egli? Mio padre!

TUTTI
Suo padre!

AMNERIS
In poter nostro!...

AIDA
Tu! Prigionier!

AMONASRO *(piano ad Aida)*
Non mi tradir!

IL RE *(ad Amonasro)*
T'appressa...Dunque tu sei?

AMONASRO
Suo padre. Anch'io pugnai,
Vinti noi fummo, morte invan cercai.

Indicating his uniform.

AIDA
What do I see? He? My father!

ALL
Her father!

AMNERIS
In our power!

AIDA
You! A prisoner!

AMONASRO *(to Aida, softly)*
Do not betray me.

THE KING *(to Amonasro)*
Come here. Now, who are you?

AMONASRO
Her father. I too fought.
We were conquered. I sought death in vain.

Quest'assisa ch'io vesto vi dica
Che il mio Re, la mia patria ho difeso:
Fu la sorte a nostr'armi nemica.
Tornò vano de' forti l'ardir.
Al mio pie' nella polve disteso
Giacque il Re da più colpi trafitto;
Se l'amor della patria è delitto
Siam rei tutti, siam pronti a morir!

This uniform is witness
that I defended my King and my country.
Fate was our enemy,
our courage was in vain.
In the dust at my feet
lay my King, dead of his wounds.
If love of one's country is a crime,
then we are all guilty, and ready to die.

turning to the King, in a pleading voice

Ma tu, Re, tu signore possente,
A costoro ti volgi clemente;
Oggi noi siam percossi dal fato,
Doman voi potria il fato colpir.

But you, O King, are a mighty lord.
Look with mercy on these captives.
Today we are laid low by fate
tomorrow, such might be your lot.

AIDA
Ma tu, Re, tu signore possente, *ecc.*

AIDA
But you, O King, are a mighty lord, *etc.*

PRIGIONIERI E SCHIAVE
Sì: dai Numi percossi noi siamo;
Tua pietà, tua clemenza imploriamo;
Ah! giammai di soffrir vi sia dato
Ciò che in oggi n'è dato soffrir! *ecc.*

SLAVE GIRLS AND PRISONERS
Yes, we are laid low by the gods,
and we beseech your mercy upon us.
Ah, may you never have to suffer
what today we are suffering! *etc.*

RAMFIS E SACERDOTI
Sturggi, o Re, queste ciurme feroci,
Chiudi il core alle perfide voci.
Fur dai numi votati alla morte,
Or de' numi si compia il voler! *ecc.*

RAMFIS AND PRIESTS
Destroy, O King, these ferocious slaves,
close your heart to their traitorous pleas,
the gods have condemned them to die,
let the will of the gods be done! *etc.*

AIDA, SCHIAVE, PRIGIONIERI
Pietà! Pietà! Pietà!

AIDA, SLAVE GIRLS AND PRISONERS
Have mercy! Have mercy! Have mercy!

POPOLO

Sacerdoti, gli sdegni placate,
L'umil prece dei vinti ascolatate;
E tu, o Re, tu possente, tu forte,
A clemenza dischiudi il pensier! *ecc.*

RAMFIS, SACERDOTI

A morte! A morte! A morte!
O Re, struggi queste ciurme, *ecc.*

SCHIAVE, PRIGIONIERI

Tua pietade, tua clemenza imploriamo, *ecc.*

RADAMÈS *(fra sè)*

Il dolor che in quel volto favella
Al mio sguardo la rende più bella;
Ogni stilla del pianto adorato
Nel mio petto ravviva l'ardor, *ecc.*

AIDA, AMONASRO *(insieme e variamente)*

Ma tu, Re, Signor possente, *ecc.*

AMNERIS *(fra sè)*

Quali sguardi sovr'essa ha rivolti!
Di qual fiamma balenano i volti!
Ed io sola, avvilita, reietta?
La vendetta mi rugge nel cor, *ecc.*

IL RE

Or che fausti ne arridon gli eventi
A costoro mostriamoci clementi;
La pietà sale ai numi gradita
E rafferma de'prenci il poter,
ecc.

POPULACE

Priests, oh calm this fury,
hear their humble prayers.
And you, O mighty king,
open your heart to mercy! *etc.*

RAMFIS AND PRIESTS

Put them to death! To death!
Destroy, O King, this rabble, *etc.*

SLAVE GIRLS AND PRISONERS

We beseech your mercy, *etc.*

RADAMÈS *(to himself)*

The grief which speaks through her eyes
makes her lovelier still in my sight.
Each tear of my beloved's eyes
deepens my love for her, *etc.*

AIDA, AMONASRO *(severally and together)*

But you, O King, are a might lord, *etc.*

AMNERIS *(to herself)*

How he looked upon her!
What flames light up their eyes!
And I—alone, abject, repulsed?
Vengeance cries out in my heart, *etc.*

THE KING

Now that fortune smiles upon us,
let us be merciful towards our victims;
for mercy is good in the sight of the gods,
mercy confirms the power of the prince,
etc.

disc no. 1/track 26 *O Re, pei sacri Numi . . . Gloria all'Egitto*

The second act comes to a stunning conclusion in an even more massive ensemble that resolves the question Amonasro raises and leaves the people in awe of the Egyptian king's mercy. Verdi reprises the "Gloria all'Egitto" chorus **(02:17)**, with the principals all voicing their feelings in the moment, and the curtain rings down with a thrilling restatement of the Triumphal March.

RADAMÈS *(al Re)*
O Re, pei sacri numi,
Per lo splendor della tua corona,
Compier giurasti il voto mio.

RADAMÈS *(turning to the King)*
O King, you swore in the name of the
gods, and by the splendour of your crown,
You swore to grant me my wish.

IL RE
Giurai.

THE KING
I have sworn.

RADAMÈS
Ebbene a te pei prigionieri etiopi
Vita domando e libertà.

RADAMÈS
Then, for the Ethiopian prisoners
I ask you for life, for freedom.

AMNERIS *(fra sè)*
Per tutti!

AMNERIS *(to herself)*
For all!

SACERDOTI
Morte ai nemici della patria!

PRIESTS
Death to the enemy!

POPOLO
Grazia per gli infelici!

POPULACE
Mercy on the wretches!

RAMFIS
Ascolta, o Re.

RAMFIS
Hear me, O King.

to Radamès

Tu pure, giovin eroe,

You too, youthful hero,

Saggio consiglio ascolta:
Son nemici e prodi sono,
La vendetta hanno nel cor;
Fatti audaci dal perdono
Correranno all'armi ancor!

RADAMÈS
Spento Amonasro, il re guerrier,
Non resta speranza ai vinti.

RAMFIS
Almeno,
Arra di pace e securtà, fra noi
Resti col padre Aida.

IL RE
Al tuo consiglio io cedo.
Di securtà, di pace un miglior pegno
Or io vo' darvi.
Radamès, la patria tutto a te deve.
D'Amneris la mano premio ti sia.
Sovra l'Egitto un giorno
Con essa regnerai...

AMNERIS (fra sè)
Venga or la schiava,
Venga a rapirmi l'amor mio...se l'osa!

IL RE, POPOLO
Gloria all'Egitto, ad Iside
Che il sacro suol difende;
S'intrecci il loto al lauro
Sul crin del vincitor! *ecc.*

hear my wise counsel.
They are the enemy and they are brave.
Their hearts are eager for revenge.
Encouraged by our mercy,
they will take up arms again!

RADAMÈS
If Amonasro the warrior king is dead,
they can no longer hope to fight us.

RAMFIS
At least,
as a pledge of peace, let Aida,
with her father, remain with us.

THE KING
I yield to your good counsel.
And now I give you a greater
pledge of peace:
Radamès, the fatherland owes everything
to you. The hand of Amneris shall be your
reward. One day, with her,
you shall rule over Egypt.

AMNERIS (to herself)
Let the slave
try to steal my love—if she dares!

THE KING AND POPULACE
Glory to Egypt and to Isis,
protectress of the sacred land.
Weave the lotus and the laurel
into a crown for the victor! *etc.*

SCHIAVE E PRIGIONIERI
Gloria al clemente Egizio
Che i nostri ceppi ha sciolto,
Che ci ridona ai liberi
Solchi del patrio suol! *ecc.*

RAMFIS E SACERDOTI
Inni leviamo ad Iside
Che il sacro suol difende;
Preghiamo che i fati arridano
Fausti alla patria ognor, *ecc.*

AIDA *(fra sè)*
Qual speme ormai più restami?
A lui la gloria e il trono...
A me l'oblio...le lacrime
Di disperato amor, *ecc.*

RADAMÈS *(fra sè)*
D'avverso nume il folgore
Sul capo mio discende...
Ah no! d'Egitto il soglio
Non val d'Aida il cor, *ecc.*

AMNERIS *(fra sè)*
Dall'inatteso giubilo
Inebriata io sono;
Tutti in un dì si compiono
I sogni del mio cor, *ecc.*

RAMFIS
Preghiam, *ecc.*

SLAVE GIRLS AND PRISONERS
Glory to merciful Egypt,
which has dissolved our bonds,
which sends us once again
to the free fields of our native land! *etc.*

RAMFIS AND PRIESTS
Let us sing hymns to Isis,
protectress of the sacred land.
Let us pray that the fates may be
forever auspicious to our nation, *etc.*

AIDA *(to herself)*
What hope now is left to me?
For him—glory and the throne,
for me—oblivion and the tears
of a hopeless love, *etc.*

RADAMÈS *(to himself)*
The lightning of an enemy god
has struck me.
Ah, no, the throne of Egypt
is not worth Aida's heart, *etc.*

AMNERIS *(to herself)*
I am intoxicated
with unforeseen joy;
in one single day, all the dreams
of my heart have come true, *etc.*

RAMFIS
Let us pray that the fates, *etc.*

IL RE, POPOLO
Gloria ad Iside, *ecc.*

AMONASRO *(ad Aida, sotto voce)*
Fa cor, della tua patria
I lievi eventi aspetta.
Per noi della vendetta
Già prossimo è l'albor, *ecc.*

POPOLO
Gloria all'Egitto, ad Iside
Che il sacro suol difende;
S'intrecci il loto al lauro
Sul crin del vincitor! *ecc.*

RADAMÈS *(fra sè)*
Qual inatteso folgore
Sul capo mio discende, *ecc.*

AMNERIS *(fra sè)*
Tutte in un dì, *ecc.*

AMONASRO *(ad Aida, sotto voce)*
Fà cor, *ecc.*

AIDA *(fra sè)*
A me l'oblio, *ecc.*

RAMFIS, SACERDOTI
Inni leviamo ad Iside, *ecc.*

SCHIAVE, PRIGIONIERI
Gloria al clemente Egizio, *ecc.*

THE KING AND POPULACE
Glory to Isis, *etc.*

AMONASRO *(toad Aida)*
Be brave, wait patiently
for happier days for our land.
For us the day of revenge
is already dawning, *etc.*

POPULACE
Glory to Egypt and to Isis,
protectress of the sacred land!
Weave the lotus and the laurel
into a crown for the victor! *etc.*

RADAMÈS *(aside)*
What an unlooked-for blow
has fallen upon my head, *etc.*

AMNERIS *(aside)*
All the dreams of my heart, *etc.*

AMONASRO *(aside to Aida)*
Be brave, *etc.*

AIDA *(aside)*
For me oblivion, *etc.*

RAMFIS AND PRIESTS
Let us sing hymns to Isis, *etc.*

SLAVE GIRLS AND PRISONERS
Glory to merciful Egypt, *etc.*

Act Three

The banks of the Nile.

Granite rocks, interspersed with palm trees. At the summit of the rocks, the Temple of Isis, half-hidden by the palms. It is a clear, starry night, a bright moon is shining.

CORO *(nel tempio)*
O tu che sei d'Osiride
Madre immortale e sposa,
Diva che i casti palpiti
Desti agli umani in cor,
Soccorri a noi pietosa,
Madre d'immenso amor! *ecc.*

CHORUS *(in the temple)*
O thou, eternal mother
and spouse of Osiris,
goddess, who dost awaken
the chaste fire in human hearts,
succor us in thy mercy,
O mother of infinite love! *etc.*

A boat draws up at the riverbank. Amneris, Ramfis, together with a group of heavily veiled women and guards, alight from the boat.

RAMFIS *(ad Amneris)*
Vieni d'Iside al tempio alla vigilia
Delle tue nozze, invoca
Della diva il favore. Iside legge
Dei mortali nel core; ogni mistero
Degli umani a lei è noto.

RAMFIS *(to Amneris)*
Come to the Temple of Isis, to beseech
the goddess's favour on the eve
of your wedding. Isis reads
in the hearts of mortals; every human
mystery is known to her.

AMNERIS
Sì: io pregherò che Radamès mi doni
Tutto il suo cor, come il mio cor a lui
Sacro è per sempre.

AMNERIS
Yes, I shall pray that Radamès give me
his whole heart, as my heart is given
in sacred love, forever, to him.

RAMFIS
Andiamo
Pregherai ai fino all'alba; io sarò teco.

RAMFIS
Let us go. You will pray until dawn. I shall
stay with you.

All enter the temple.

CORO
Soccorri a noi pietosa, *ecc.*

CHORUS
Succor us in thy mercy, *etc.*

Aida enters furtively. She is veiled.

disc no. 2/track 4 *O patria mia* After entering the Temple of Isis and wondering aloud why
Radamès has asked to meet her here, Aida begins her great aria in which she
longs for the bewitching atmosphere of her native land. The musical style here is
tender, rapt, and lyrically passionate **(00:18)**, very different from the declamatory
grit of "Ritorna vincitor!" Few sopranos encompass both extremes of expression,
especially given what Verdi asks for at the end of this aria. The soprano must
rise to a fearsomely exposed high C **(03:48)**, and then finish the aria in an enormously difficult winding phrase, embellished by the woodwinds.

AIDA
Qui Radamès verrà! Che vorrà dirmi?
Io tremo. Ah! se tu vieni
A recarmi, o crudel, l'ultimo addio,
Del Nilo i cupi vortici
Mi daran tomba, e pace forse, e oblìo.
O patria mia, mai più ti rivedrò!
O cieli azzurri, o dolci aure native,
Dove sereno il mio mattin brillò,
O verdi colli, o profumate rive,
O patria mia, mai più ti rivedrò! *ecc.*
O fresche valli, o queto asil beato,
Che un dì promesso dall'amor mi fu;

AIDA
Radamès will come here. What will he say?
I tremble. Ah! If you come, cruel man,
to bid me a last farewell, in the dark eddies
of the Nile I shall find my tomb, perhaps
peace—but at least, oblivion! O fatherland,
I shall never see you again! O blue skies,
soft breezes of my homeland, where I lived
out the quiet morning of my life, O grassy
hills, O fragrant streams, O fatherland, I
shall never see you again! *etc.* O cool valleys, blessed, peaceful haven, one day
promised me by love, now that the dream

Or che d'amore il sogno è dileguato,
O patria mia, non ti vedrò mai più! *ecc.*

Amonasro enters.

Ciel! mio padre!

AMONASRO
A te grave cagion
M'adduce, Aida.
Nulla sfugge al mio sguardo.
D'amor ti struggi
Per Radamès, ei t'ama, e lo attendi.
Dei Faraon la figlia è tua rivale...
Razza infame, aborrita e a noi fatale!

AIDA
E in suo potere io sto!
Io, d'Amonasro figlia!

AMONASRO
In poter di lei!
No! se lo brami
La possente rival tu vincerai.
E patria, e trono, e amor, tutto tu avrai.
Riverdrai le foreste imbalsamate,
Le fresche valli, i nostri templi d'or.

of love is gone, O fatherland, I shall never
see you again! *etc.*

Heaven! My father!

AMONASRO
A grave matter has brought me here, Aida.
Nothing escapes my eyes.
Love for Radamès is killing you.
He loves you too. You are waiting for him.
The daughter of the Pharaohs is your
rival—Princess of a hated race, our deadly
enemy.

AIDA
And I am in her power!
I, the daughter of Amonasro!

AMONASRO
In her power!
No! if you wish, you can defeat your powerful rival, and fatherland, throne, and love
will all be yours. You will see again our fragrant forests, the cool valleys and the gold-
en temples.

disc no. 2/track 6 *Riverdrai le foreste imbalsamente* Amonasro's unexpected arrival leads
to this duet, which emerges in three distinct sections: the Ethiopian king gently
reaches out to his daughter; then bluntly insists she remember the way Egypt has
devastated her homeland; only for her to respond by begging wearily for peace.
Verdi reflects the interplay of their mixed motives: as Amonasro's fanatical sense

of revenge tightens in strident, chilling orchestral effects **(02:34)**, Aida seems to drift further and further from reality, and her music becomes increasingly ethereal **(03:46)**

AIDA
Rivedrò le foreste imbalsamate,
Le fresche valli, i nostri templi d'or.

AMONASRO
Sposa felice a lui che amasti tanto,
Tripudii immensi ivi potrai gioir.

AIDA
Un giorno solo di sì ce incanto,
Un'ora di tal gioia, e poi morir!

AMONASRO
Pur rammenti che a noi l'Egizio immite,
Le case, i templi e l'are profanò,
Trasse in ceppi le vergini rapite;
Madri, vecchi,
Fanciulli ei trucidò.

AIDA
Ah! ben rammento, quegl'infausti giorni!
Rammento i lutti che il mio cor soffrì.
Deh, fate, o Numi,
che per noi ritorni
L'alba invocata de' sereni dì.

AMONASRO
Rammenta...
Non fia che tardi.
In armi ora si desta

AIDA
I shall see again our fragrant forests,
the cool valleys and the golden temples.

AMONASRO
Happy bride of the one you love,
you shall know great joys at last.

AIDA
One day of such enchantment
one hour of such great joy—then I can die!

AMONASRO
You have not forgotten that pitiless Egypt
defiled our altars, temples, and homes,
carrying off our maidens in slavery,
murdering our mothers, our old men,
and our children?

AIDA
Ah, I remember well those unhappy days,
and the mournful sorrow which filled my
heart. Ah, grant, O gods, that for us may
return the dawn of those peaceful days for
which we pray.

AMONASRO
Remember...
It cannot be long delayed.
Our people even now are ready for battle;

Il popol nostro; tutto è pronto già,
Vittoria avrem. Solo a saper mi resta
Qual sentiero il nemico seguirà.

AIDA
Chi scoprirlo potria? chi mai?

AMONASRO
Tu stessa!

AIDA
Io!

AMONASRO
Radamès so che qui attendi...Ei t'ama...
Ei conduce gli Egizii...
Intendi?

AIDA
Orrore!
Che mi consigli tu? No! no! giammai!

AMONASRO *(con impeto selvaggio)*
Su, dunque! sorgete,
Egizie coorti!
Col fuoco struggete
Le nostre città.
Spargete il terrore,
Le stragi, le morti.
Al vostro furore
Più freno non v'ha.

all is prepared, and we shall conquer.
One thing is lacking—for me to know
the route that the enemy will follow.

AIDA
Who could find out? Who?

AMONASRO
You could!

AIDA
I!

AMONASRO
I know you are waiting for Radamès. He
loves you. He is the Egyptian captain.
Do you understand?

AIDA
A horrid thought!
What are you asking of me? No, never!

AMONASRO *(fiercely)*
Arise then
soldiers of Egypt!
Sack and burn
our cities!
Spread terror,
rape, and death!
There is no rein now
to your fury!

AIDA
Ah padre!

AMONASRO *(respingendola)*
Mia figlia ti chiami!

AIDA
Pietà!

AMONASRO
Flutti di sangue scorrono
Sulle città dei vinti.
Vedi? dai negri vortici
Si levano gli estinti.
Ti additan essi e gridano
Per te la patria muor!

AIDA
Pietà! Ah padre, pietà!

AMONASRO
Una larva orribile
Fra l'ombre e noi s'affaccia.
Trema! le scarne braccia
Sul capo tuo levò.
Tua madre ell'è, ravvisala
Ti maledice...

AIDA *(nel massimo terrore)*
Ah! padre! no!...Ah! pietà, padre!, *ecc.*

AMONASRO *(respingendola)*
Non sei mia figlia!
Dei Faraoni tu sei la schiava!

AIDA
Ah father! father!

AMONASRO *(repulsing her)*
You call yourself my daughter!

AIDA
Have pity!

AMONASRO
Waves of blood are flowing
over the vanquished cities.
See—from the black swirls
the dead arise.
They point at you and cry,
"Because of you, our country dies!"

AIDA
Have pity! Father, have pity!

AMONASRO
A horrid spectre
rises in the shadows before us.
Tremble, for over your head
it lifts its bony arms.
It is your mother—see her,
she is cursing you!

AIDA *(terrified)*
Ah! father! no! have pity! *etc.*

AMONASRO *(repulsing her)*
You are not my daughter!
You are the slave of the Pharaohs!

AIDA
Ah! Pietà! Pietà!
Padre, a costoro schiava non sono;
Non maledirmi, non imprecarmi;
Ancor tua figlia potrai chiamarmi,
Della mia patria degna sarò.

AMONASRO
Pensa che un popolo vinto, straziato,
Per te solitanto risorger può...

AIDA
O patria! o patria...quanto mi
costi!

AMONASRO
Coraggio! ei giunge, là tutto
udrò.

AIDA
Ah! Have pity! Have pity!
Father, I am not their slave.
Do not curse me nor revile me—
you will call me daughter again,
for I shall be worthy of my country.

AMONASRO
Remember that a whole people, conquered
and suffering, can rise again through you!

AIDA
O fatherland, what a price I must pay, for
thee!

AMONASRO
Be brave! He is coming now. I shall hear
all.

He hides among the palms. Radamès enters.

RADAMÈS
Pur ti reveggo, mia dolce Aida...

AIDA
T'arresta, vanne, che speri
ancor?

RADAMÈS
A te dappresso l'amor mi guida.

AIDA
Te i riti attendono d'un altro amor.
D'Amneris sposo...

RADAMÈS
At last I am with you again, sweet Aida.

AIDA
Stop, go away! What do you want from
me?

RADAMÈS
It is love which brings me to you.

AIDA
But the rites of another love await you.
Married to Amneris—

RADAMÈS
Che parli mai?
Te sola, Aida, te deggio amar.
Gli dei m'ascoltano,
 tu mia sarai.

AIDA
D'uno spergiuro non ti macchiar!
Prode t'amai, non t'amerei spergiuro.

RADAMÈS
Dell'amor mio dubiti, Aida?

AIDA
E come speri sottrarti d'Amneris ai vezzi,
Del Re al voler, del tuo popolo ai voti,
Dei sacerdoti all'ira?

RADAMÈS
Odimi, Aida.
Nel fiero anelito di nuova guerra
Il suolo etiope si ridestò;
Il tuo già invadono la nostra terra,
Io degli Egizi duce sarò.
Fra il suon, fra i plausi della vittoria,
Al Re mi prostro, gli svelo il cor;
Sarai tu il serto della mia gloria,
Vivrem beati d'eterno amore.

AIDA
Nè d'Amneris paventi
Il vindice furor? La sua vendetta,
Come folgor tremenda,
Cadrà su me, sul padre mio, su tutti.

RADAMÈS
What are you saying?
You, Aida, are the only one I can love.
As the gods are my witness, you shall be
mine.

AIDA
Do not break your oath! As a hero
I loved you, if you swear false, I cannot.

RADAMÈS
Do you doubt my love, Aida?

AIDA
But how can you escape from Amneris's
wiles, from the King's command, from the
people's will, from the wrath of the priests?

RADAMÈS
Hear me, Aida.
Ethiopia has awakened,
eager for fierce, new battles.
Your people have already invaded,
and I shall lead the Egyptians again.
Then, in the midst of the triumph,
kneeling before the king, I shall open my
heart. You shall be my victor's wreath;
and we shall live, blessed by undying love.

AIDA
And do you not fear
Amneris's wrath? Her vengeance,
like a thunderbolt,
will strike me, my father, and my people.

RADAMÈS
Io vi difendo.

AIDA
Invan, tu nol potresti.
Pur, se tu m'ami, ancor s'apre una via
Di scampo a noi...

RADAMÈS
Quale?

AIDA
Fuggir...

RADAMÈS
Fuggire!

RADAMÈS
I shall defend you.

AIDA
It would be in vain.
Yet, if you love me, there is still
an escape for us.

RADAMÈS
What is it?

AIDA
To flee—

RADAMÈS
To flee!

---

disc no. 2/track 9   *Fuggiam gli ardori inospiti . . . Là, tra foreste vergini*   Radamès's enthusiasm, echoed in the trim melodies with which he has entered the scene, is dampened by Aida's belief that their only hope is to flee to Ethiopia. She sounds desperate, swooning, as she tries to seduce him with images of the virgin forests of her homeland in an edgy melody that rises and falls chromatically **(00:40)**. This section of their encounter builds the momentum that leads to the fateful exchange in which Radamès is betrayed.

AIDA
Fuggiam gli arbori inospiti
Di queste lande ignude;
Una novella patria
Al nostro amor si schiude.
Là...tra foreste vergini,
Di fiori profumate,

AIDA
Let us flee from the scorching sun
of this desert land.
A new fatherland
reveals itself to our love.
There, in the virgin forests,
fragrant with sweet flowers, we shall forget

In estasi beate
La terra scorderem.

RADAMÈS
Sovra una terra estrania
Teco fuggir dovrei!
Abbandonar la patria
L'are de' nostri dei!
Il suol dov'io raccolsi
Di gloria i primi allori,
Il ciel de'nostri amori
Come scordar potrem?

AIDA
Là tra foreste vergini, *ecc.*

the world
in blessed joy.

RADAMÈS
You asked me to flee with you
to a foreign land?
To abandon my fatherland
and the altars of our gods?
This land where I first plucked
the flowers of glory,
this land where first we loved—
how can we forget it?

AIDA
There, in the virgin forest, *etc.*

JON VICKERS AS RADAMÈS
IN 1961.

RADAMÈS
Le ciel dei nostri amori, *ecc.*

AIDA
Sotto il mio ciel, più libero
L'amor ne fia concesso;
Ivi nel tempio istesso
Gli stessi numi avrem, *ecc.*

RADAMÈS
Abbandonar la patria, *ecc.*

AIDA
Fuggiam, fuggiam!

RADAMÈS *(esitante)*
Aida!

AIDA
Tu non m'ami...Va!

RADAMÈS
Non t'amo?

AIDA
No!

RADAMÈS
Mortal giammai né dio
Arse d'amor al par del mio possente.

AIDA
Va, va, t'attende all'ara
Amneris.

RADAMÈS
The land where first we loved, *etc.*

AIDA
Beneath my country's freer skies
it will be granted to us to love.
There, in the same temples
we shall worship the same gods, *etc.*

RADAMÈS
To abandon my fatherland, *etc.*

AIDA
Let us flee—

RADAMÈS *(hesitating)*
Aida!

AIDA
You do not love me—go!

RADAMÈS
Not love you!

AIDA
No!

RADAMÈS
No man, no god
has ever burned with such a love!

AIDA
Go, go—Amneris is waiting for you
at the altar—

RADAMÈS

No! Giammai!

AIDA

Giammai, dicesti?
Allor piombi la scure
Su me, sul padre mio...

RADAMÈS

Ah no! fuggiamo!
Sì, fuggiam da queste mura,
Al deserto insiem fuggiamo;
Qui sol regna la sventura,
Là si schiude un ciel d'amor.
I deserti interminati
A noi talamo saranno
Su noi gli astri brilleranno
Di più limpido fulgor.

AIDA

Nella terra avventurata
De' miei padri il ciel ne attende:
Ivi l'aura è imbalsamata,
Ivi il suolo è aromi e fior.
Fresche valli e verdi prati
A noi talamo saranno,
Su noi gli astri brillerano
Di più limpido fulgor.

AIDA E RADAMÈS

Vieni meco, insiem fuggiamo
Questa terra di dolor.
Vieni meco, t'amo, t'amo!
A noi duce fia l'amor.

RADAMÈS

No, never!

AIDA

Never, you say?
Then the headsman's axe will fall
on me, on my father—

RADAMÈS

Ah no! Let us flee together.
Yes, let us flee, far from these walls,
let us flee, together, to the desert.
Here there is nothing but misfortune,
there we shall find a heaven of love.
The never-ending desert
will be our wedding bed,
the stars will shine upon us
with a purer, brighter light!

AIDA

In the happy land
of my fathers, heaven awaits us.
There the breeze blows sweet
over that perfumed land of flowers.
Cool valleys and green fields
will be our wedding bed.
The stars will shine upon us
with a purer, brighter light!

AIDA AND RADAMÈS

Come with me, we shall flee together,
from this land of sorrow.
Come with me, I love you,
and love shall be our king.

AIDA
Ma, dimmi: per qual via
Eviterem le schiere degli armati?

RADAMÈS
Il sentier scelto dai nostri
A piombar sul nemico fia deserto
Fino a domani.

AIDA
E quel sentier?

RADAMÈS
Le gole di Nápata.

Amonasro comes forward.

AMONASRO
Di Nàpata le gole!
Ivi saranno i miei!

RADAMÈS
Oh! chi ci ascolta?

AMONASRO
D'Aida il padre e degli Etiopi il Re.

RADAMÈS *(agitatissimo)*
Tu, Amonasro!...tu, il Re?
Numi! che dissi?
No!...non è ver!...sogno...
Delirio è questo...

AIDA
But tell me—how can we avoid
the Egyptian legions?

RADAMÈS
The route by which my men
will march against the enemy
will be free until tomorrow.

AIDA
And that route is?

RADAMÈS
The pass of Napata.

AMONASRO
The pass of Napata!
My men will be there!

RADAMÈS
Who has overheard us?

AMONASRO
Aida's father, the King of the Ethiopians!

RADAMÈS *(excitedly)*
You—Amonasro! You—the King! O gods!
What have I done?
No, it cannot be, it cannot be!
I dream! I am raving mad!

AIDA
Ah no! ti calma...ascoltami,
All'amor mio t'affida

AMONASRO
A te l'amor d'Aida
Un soglio innalzerà.

RADAMÈS
Io son disonorato!
Per te tradi la patria

AIDA
Ti calma!

AMONASRO
No tu non sei colpevole,
Era voler del fato.

RADAMÈS
Io son disonorato!

AIDA
Ah! no!

RADAMÈS
Per te tradi la patria!

AMONASRO
No tu non se colpevole.

AIDA
Ti calma...

AIDA
Ah no! Be calm. Listen to me,
trust in my love.

AMONASRO
Aida's love for you
will build you a throne!

RADAMÈS
I am dishonoured! Dishonoured!
For you I have betrayed my country!

AIDA
Be calm!

AMONASRO
No! You are not guilty,
it was the will of Fate.

RADAMÈS
I am dishonoured!

AIDA
Ah, no!

RADAMÈS
For you I have betrayed my country!

AMONASRO
No: you are not guilty.

AIDA
Be calm...

AMONASRO
Vieni: oltre il Nil ne attendono
I prodi a noi devoti;
Là del tu core i voti
Coronerà l'amor.
Vieni!

AMONASRO
Come—beyond the Nile
my brave and faithful men are waiting.
There, love shall fulfill
the wishes of your heart.
Come!

Amneris, Ramfis, the priests, and guards come out from the temple.

AMNERIS
Traditor!

AMNERIS
Traitor!

AIDA
La mia rival!...

AIDA
My rival!

AMONASRO *(avventandosi su Amneris con un pugnale)*
L'opra mia a strugger vieni!
Muori!

AMONASRO *(throwing himself upon Amneris with drawn dagger)*
You have come to defeat my plans.
You shall die!

RADAMÈS *(frapponendosi)*
Arresta, insano!

RADAMÈS *(coming between them)*
Stop, madman!

AMONASRO
Oh rabbia!

AMONASRO
Oh, fury!

RAMFIS
Guardie, olà!

RAMFIS
Guards, look out!

RADAMÈS *(ad Aida ed Amonasro)*
Presto! fuggite!

RADAMÈS *(to Aida and Amonasro)*
Quickly! Flee!

AMONASRO *(trascinando Aida)*
Vieni, o figlia!

AMONASRO *(dragging Aida)*
Come, my daughter.

RAMFIS *(alle guardie)*
Li inseguite!

RADAMÈS *(a Ramfis)*
Sacerdote, io resto a te.

RAMFIS *(to the guards)*
After them!

RADAMÈS *(to Ramfis)*
Priest, I am in your hands.

Act Four

Scene One

A hall in the King's palace.

*Left, a great door leading to the underground judgment chamber. A passage,
right, leads to Radamès's cell.*

AMNERIS *(mestamente atteggiata davanti la porta
del sotteraneo)*
L'aborrita rivale a me sfuggia...
Dai sacerdoti Radamès attende
Dei traditor la pena. Traditor
Egli non è. Pur rivelò di guerra
L'alto segreto. Egli fuggir volea,
Con lei fuggire! Traditori tutti!
A morte! A morte!
Oh! che mai parlo? Io l'amo,
Io l'amo sempre. Disperato, insano
È quest'amor che la mia vita strugge.
Oh! s'ei potesse amarmi!
Vorrei salvarlo. E come?
Si tenti! Guardie, Radamès qui venga.

AMNERIS *(sadly, standing before the door)*
My hated rival has escaped.
Radamès awaits, from the hands
of the priests, the traitor's punishment.
But he is not a traitor,
even if he revealed the secret plan.
He meant to flee—with her!
Traitors all! Death to them—death!
Oh, what am I saying? I love him,
I still love him, with a mad, a desperate
love, which is killing me.
Oh! if only he might love me!
I should like to save him. How? I shall try!
Guards,
bring Radamès to me.

Radamès enters, escorted by guards.

Giá i sacerdoti adunansi
Arbitri del tuo fato;
Pur dell'accusa orribile
Scolparti ancor t'è dato;
Ti scolpa e la tua grazia

The priests even now are in counsel,
deciding your fate.
But you can still establish your innocence
in answer to the dread accusations.
Clear yourself, and I shall ask

Io pregherò dal trono,
E nunzia di perdono,
Di vita a te sarò.

RADAMÈS
Di mie discolpe i giudici
Mai non udran l'accento;
Dinanzi ai numi, agl'uomini
Né vil, né reo mi sento.
ProffeRse il labbro incauto
Fatal segreto, è vero,
Ma puro il mio pensiero
E l'onor mio restò.

AMNERIS
Salvati dunque e scolpati.

RADAMÈS
No.

AMNERIS
Tu morrai.

RADAMÈS
La vita
Aborro! d'ogni gaudio
La fonte inaridita
Svanita ogni speranza,
Sol bramo di morir.

AMNERIS
Morire! Ah, tu dêi vivere!
Sì, all'amor mio vivrai;
Per te le angosce orribili

pardon for you from the King.
In that way, I can bring
both pardon and life to you.

RADAMÈS
The judges shall never hear me
try to defend myself.
Before the gods and man
I feel myself neither traitorous nor guilty.
My incautious words
revealed the secret, it is true.
But both my thought
and my honour remain unstained by guilt.

AMNERIS
Then defend yourself—save yourself.

RADAMÈS
No.

AMNERIS
You will die—

RADAMÈS
Life
is hateful to me. The source
of all joy is now dry,
every hope is gone.
I wish only to die.

AMNERIS
To die! Ah, you must live!
Yes, you shall live my love.
For you, I have already felt

Di morte io già provai;
T'amai, soffersi tanto,
Vegliai le notti in pianto,
E patria, e trono, e vita
Tutto darei per te.

RADAMÈS
Per essa anch'io lo patria
E l'onor mio tradia...

AMNERIS
Di lei non più!

RADAMÈS
L'infamia
Mi attende e vuoi ch'io viva?
Misero appien mi festi,
Aida a me togliesti;
Spenta l'hai forse, e in dono
Offri la vita a me?

AMNERIS
Io, di sua morte origine!
No, vive Aida!

RADAMÈS
Vive!

AMNERIS
Nei diperati aneliti
Dell'orde fuggitive
Sol cadde il padre.

the horrible anguish of death.
I loved, I suffered,
I passed the nights in tears.
My country, my throne, my life—
I should give up all for you.

RADAMÈS
For her, I too betrayed
My country and my honour.

AMNERIS
Do not speak of her!

RADAMÈS
Infamy
is my lot—and you ask me to live?
You brought me to the depths of misery,
you took Aida from me.
Perhaps, because of you, she is dead—
and you offer me my life?

AMNERIS
Aida is dead, because of me?
No, she is alive!

RADAMÈS
She is alive!

AMNERIS
In the desperate flight
of the fleeing hordes
only her father died.

RADAMÈS
Ed ella?

AMNERIS
Sparve, né più novella
S'ebbe...

RADAMÈS
Gli dei l'adducano
Salva alle patrie mura,
E ignori la sventura
Di chi per le morrà!

AMNERIS
Or, s'io ti salvo, giurami
Che più non la vedrai...

RADAMÈS
Nol posso!

AMNERIS
A lei rinunzia
Per sempre, e tu vivrai!

RADAMÈS
Nol posso!

AMNERIS
Ancor una volta
A lei rinunzia.

RADAMÈS
È vano.

RADAMÈS
And she?

AMNERIS
She disappeared,
nothing is known of her.

RADAMÈS
May the gods lead her
safely to her home.
May she never know the fate
of the one who will die for her!

AMNERIS
If I save you, swear to me
that you will never see her again.

RADAMÈS
I cannot!

AMNERIS
If you renounce her
forever, you will live!

RADAMÈS
I cannot!

AMNERIS
Once more—
renounce her.

RADAMÈS
It is in vain.

AMNERIS
Morir vuoi dunque, insano?

RADAMÈS
Pronto a morir son già.

AMNERIS
Chi ti salva, sciagurato,
Dalla sorte che t'aspetta?
In furor hai tu cangiato
Un amor ch'egual non ha.
De' miei pianti la vendetta
Ora dal ciel compirà, *ecc.*

RADAMÈS
È la morte un ben supremo
Se per lei morir m'è dato;
Nel subir l'estrmo fato
Gaudi immensi il core avrà;
L'ira umana più non temo,
Temo sol la tua pietà, *ecc.*

AMNERIS
Ah! chi ti salva?...
De' miei pianti, *ecc.*

AMNERIS
Madman—you insist on dying?

RADAMÈS
I am ready to die!

AMNERIS
Who will save you, wretch,
from the fate that awaits you?
You have changed into hatred
a love which had no equal.
Only heaven
can now avenge my tears, *etc.*

RADAMÈS
Death is the greatest good,
if I may die for her;
in going to meet my fate
my heart will know great joy;
I have no fear of mortal wrath,
your pity is the only thing I fear, *etc.*

AMNERIS
Ah, who will save him?…
Only heaven, *etc.*

Radamès exits, surrounded by guards.

disc no. 2/track 13 *Ohimè! Morir mi sento!*

After a tragic encounter between the doomed Radamès and the heartbroken Amneris, the rest of the first scene of Act IV **(running through track 15)** is known as the Judgment Scene. It primarily provides a tour de force for the mezzo-soprano singing Amneris, who is onstage constantly. The questioning of Radamès and the deliberations of the priests take place offstage, with the entire drama reflected in Amneris's response. When the penalty of death is handed down to Radamès, Amneris is like a caged animal **(track 15, 00:04)**; she explodes at the priests in a fury **(track 15, 02:28)**, capping her anger with a blazing-high B-flat.

Left RITA GORR, MEZZO-SOPRANO, AS AMNERIS.

Following page A 1994 PRODUCTION OF AIDA AT THE LYRIC OPERA OF CHICAGO.

AMNERIS *(cade desolata su di un sedile)*
Ohimè! morir mi sento!
Oh! chi lo salva?
E in poter di costoro
Io stessa lo gettai! Ora a te impreco,
Atroce gelosia, che la sua morte
Ei il lutto eterno del mio cor segnasti!

She turns and sees the priests, descending into Radamès's underground prison.

Ecco i fatali,
Gl'inesorati ministri di morte!
Oh! ch'io non vegga quelle bianche larve!

She covers her face with her hands.

E in poter di costoro
Io stessa lo gettai! *ecc.*

RAMFIS E SACERDOTI *(nel sotteraneo)*
Spirto del nume, sovra noi discendi!
Ne avviva al raggio dell'eterna luce;
Pel labbro nostro tua giustizia apprendi.

AMNERIS
Numi, pietà del mio straziato core...
Egli è innocente, lo salvate, o Numi!
Disperato, tremendo è il mio dolore!

RAMFIS E SACERDOTI
Spirto del Nume, *ecc.*

AMNERIS *(desolate, she falls into a chair)*
Alas! I shall die!
Oh, who will save him?
And it was I who cast him
into their hands! Now I curse
my jealousy, which brought his death
and eternal mourning in my heart!

Ah, there they are—
the pitiless ministers of death!
Oh, may I not see them, these white-robed ghouls!

And it was I who cast him
into their hands! *etc.*

RAMFIS AND PRIESTS *(in the vault)*
Spirit of the gods, descend upon us!
Let thy eternal ray enlighten us;
let our lips pronounce thy justice.

AMNERIS
O gods, take pity on my anguished heart!
He is innocent—save him, O gods!
My grief is desperate, overwhelming!

RAMFIS AND PRIESTS
Spirit of the gods, *etc.*

AMNERIS

Oh, chi lo salva? Mi sento morir!

AMNERIS

Oh, who will save him? I shall die!

Radamès, surrounded by guards, is led into the vault. Amneris, seeing him cries out.

RAMFIS *(nel sotterraneo)*

Radamès, Radamès, Radamès:
Tu rivelasti
Della patria i segreti allo straniero!
Discolpati!

RAMFIS *(in the vault)*

Radamès, Radamès, Radamès!
You revealed
your country's secrets to the enemy!
Defend yourself.

SACERDOTI

Discolpati!

PRIESTS

Defend yourself.

RAMFIS

Egli tace...

RAMFIS

He is silent.

TUTTI

Traditor!

ALL

Traitor!

AMNERIS

Ah, pietà! Egli è innocente! Numi, pietà!

AMNERIS

Ah, pity! He is innocent! Pity, O gods!

RAMFIS

Radamès, Radamès, Radamès:
Tu disertasti
Dal campo il dì che precedea la pugna.
Discolpati!

RAMFIS

Radamès! Radamès! Radamès!
You deserted
your command on the eve of battle.
Defend yourself.

SACERDOTI

Discolpati

PRIESTS

Defend yourself.

RAMFIS

Egli tace...

RAMFIS

He is silent.

TUTTI
Traditor!

AMNERIS
Ah, pietà! Ah, lo salvate, Numi, pietà!

RAMFIS
Radamès, Radamès, Radamès:
Tua fè violasti,
Alla patria spergiuro, al Re, all'onore.
Discolpati!

SACERDOTI
Discolpati!

RAMFIS
Egli tace...

TUTTI
Traditor!

AMNERIS
Ah, pietà! Ah, lo salvate, Numi, pietà!

RAMFIS E SACERDOTI
Radamès, è deciso il tuo fato
Degl'infami la morte tu avrai;
Sotto l'ara del Nume sdegnato
A te vivo fia schiuso l'avel.

AMNERIS
A lui vivo, la tomba! Oh! gl'infami!
Né di sangue son paghi giammai...
E si chiaman ministri del ciel!

ALL
Traitor!

AMNERIS
Ah, pity! Ah, save him! Pity, O gods!

RAMFIS
Radamès! Radamès! Radamès!
You betrayed your country, your King,
your honour.
Defend yourself

PRIESTS
Defend yourself.

RAMFIS
He is silent.

ALL
Traitor!

AMNERIS
Ah, pity! Ah, save him! Pity, O gods!

RAMFIS AND PRIESTS
Radamès, your fate is decided
you shall die a traitor's death.
Beneath the altar of the offended god,
you, living, shall be entombed.

AMNERIS
Entombed alive! Oh, the villains!
Their thirst for blood is never appeased—
yet they call themselves heaven's ministers!

RAMFIS E SACERDOTI
Traditor!

AMNERIS (*investendo i sacerdoti che escono dal sotterraneo*)
Sacerdoti: compiste un delitto!
Tigri infami di sangue asssetate
Voi la terra ed i Numi oltraggiate,
Voi punite chi colpa non ha.

RAMFIS E SACERDOTI
E traditor! morrà!

AMNERIS (*a Ramfis*)
Sacerdote: quest'uomo che uccidi,
Tu lo sai, da me un giorno fu amato,
L'anatèma d'un core straziato
Col suo sangue su te ricadrà!
Voi la terra ed i numi, *ecc.*
Ah no, non è traditor…pietà, *ecc.*

RAMFIS E SACERDOTI
E traditor! morrà!

They go out, slowly.

AMNERIS
Empia razza! anatèma su voi!
La vendetta del ciel scenderà!

RAMFIS AND PRIESTS
Traitor!

AMNERIS (*assailing the priests as they come up from the vault*)
Priests—you have committed a crime!
Infamous, bloodthirsty beasts—
you outrage the gods and man,
punishing the innocent!

RAMFIS AND PRIESTS
He is a traitor! He shall die!

AMNERIS (*to Ramfis*)
Priest, this man whom you send to death,
you know well, I once loved.
The curses of a broken heart,
together with his blood, will fall upon you!
You outrage the gods, *etc.*
Ah, he is no traitor…have mercy, *etc.*

RAMFIS AND PRIESTS
He is a traitor! He shall die.

AMNERIS
Impious brood! My curse upon you!
Heaven's vengeance will strike you!

Scene Two   *Interior of the temple of Vulcan and Radamès's tomb.*

The scene is divided into two levels. The upper part, resplendent with gold and light, represents the interior of the Temple of Vulcan; the lower level, a vault. Long rows of arches disappear into the darkness. Colossal statues of Osiris, hands crossed, hold up the pilasters of the vault. Radamès is seated on the steps by which he has descended into the vault. Above, two priests are carefully replacing the stone that closes the vault.

RADAMÈS
La fatal pietra sovra me si chiuse.
Ecco la tomba mia. Del dì la luce
Più non vedrò. Non rivedrò più Aida.
Aida, ove se tu? Possa tu almeno
Viver felice e la mia sorte orrenda
Sempre ignorar!—Qual gemito!...
Una larva... Una vision...No! forma umana
è questa... Ciel!...Aida!

AIDA
Son io.

RADAMÈS
Tu, in questa tomba!

AIDA
Presago il core della tua condanna,
In questa tomba che per te s'apriva
Io penetrai furtiva,
E qui lontana da ogni umano sguardo
Nelle tue braccia desiai morire.

RADAMÈS
Morir! si pura e bella!
Morir per me d'amore...
Degli anni tuoi nel fiore

RADAMÈS
The fatal stone has closed above me.
This is my tomb. Never again shall I see
the light of day, nor see Aida.
Aida—where are you? May you at least
live happily, never knowing
My horrid fate. A sigh? A ghost,
a vision—no, this is a human form!
Heaven!—Aida!

AIDA
Yes, I.

RADAMÈS
You, in this tomb!

AIDA
In my heart, I sensed your fate.
Secretly I came into this tomb
opened to receive you.
And here, far from every human eye,
I have chosen to die with you!

RADAMÈS
To die—so pure, so lovely!
To die, for love of me!
In the flowering of your youth,

Fuggir la vita!
T'avea il cielo per l'amor creata,
Ed io l'uccido per averti amata!
No, non morrai!
Troppo t'amai!
Troppo sei bella!

to give up your life!
Heaven created you for love,
yet I in loving you have killed you!
No, you shall not die!
I have loved you too much,
you are too lovely to die!

AIDA *(vaneggiando)*
Vedi? Di morte l'angelo
Radiante a noi s'appressa;
Ne adduce a eterni gaudii
Sovra i suoi vanni d'or.
Già veggo il ciel dischiudersi,
Ivi ogni affanno cessa,
Ivi cominicia l'estasi
D'un immortale amor.

AIDA *(in a delirium)*
See? The angel of death,
with shining wings, comes near,
to bear us to eternal joys
upon his golden wings.
Above us heaven is opening.
There, every sorrow ends,
and there joy begins,
the joy of immortal love.

*From above, the hymns of the priests and priestesses invoking
the gods can be heard.*

SACERDOTI E SACERDOTESSE
Immenso Fthà, del mondo
Spirito animator, ah!
Noi t'invochiam!

PRIESTS AND PRIESTESSES
Great Phtha, life-giving
spirit of the world, ah!
We invoke thee!

AIDA
Triste canto!

AIDA
How sad a song!

RADAMÈS
Il tripudio dei sacerdoti.

RADAMÈS
The joy of the priests!

AIDA
Il nostro inno di morte.

AIDA
Our funeral hymn.

RADAMÈS *(cercando di smuovere la pietra del sotteraneo)*
Né le mie forti braccia
Smuoverti potranno, o fatal pietra!

AIDA
In van! tutto è finito
Sulla terra per noi.

RADAMÈS *(con desolata rassegnazione)*
È vero! è vero!

RADAMÈS *(trying to move the stone that closes the vault)*
Nor does my strength suffice
to move thee, O fatal stone!

AIDA
It is useless! On earth,
all is finished for us.

RADAMÈS *(with sad resignation)*
It is true!

He comes back to Aida, to sustain her.

disc no. 2/track 18 *O terra addio* Together again at last, with death imminent, Radamès and Aida leave behind the strife of earthly life. Verdi gives them a luminous, ethereal duet that begins with an unforgettable, gently vaulting melodic phrase that is heard repeatedly. As death closes in, the duet shimmers and floats in a kind of quiet ecstasy, as the priests drone on above **(02:20)**. This final duet is perhaps the most disarming aspect of Verdi's score—after all the pomp and circumstance, the work ends with two souls bound forever in eternity, their voices evaporating in the stillness of death as the grieving Amneris prays for peace **(03:01)**.

AIDA
O terra, addio; addio, valle di pianti...
Sogno di gaudio che in dolor svanì.
A noi si schiude il ciel e l'alme erranti
Volano al raggio dell'eterno dì, *ecc.*

AIDA
O Earth, farewell—farewell, vale of tears,
dream of joy which vanished into sorrow.
Heaven opens to us, our wandering souls
fly fast towards the light of eternal day, *etc.*

AIDA E RADAMÈS
O terra addio, *ecc.*
Ah! si schiude il ciel, *ecc.*
O terra, addio, *ecc…*

AIDA AND RAMDAMES
O Earth, farewell, *etc.*
Ah! Heaven opens for us, *etc.*
O Earth, farewell, *etc…*

SACERDOTI E SACERDOTESSE
Immenso Fthà, *ecc.*

PRIESTS AND PRIESTESSES
Mighty Phtha, *etc.*

Aida sinks into the arms of Radamès. Amneris enters the temple, dressed in mourning, and prostrates herself on the stone that seals the vault.

THE FINAL ACT OF A 1963 PRODUCTION AT THE METROPOLITAN OPERA.

AMNERIS

Pace t'imploro! Salma adorata
Isi placata ti schiuda il ciel!
Pace t'imploro!
Pace, pace, pace!

AIDA E RADAMÈS

...O terra addio, *ecc.*
Si schiude il ciel!

SACERDOTI E SACERDOTESSE

Immenso Fthà!

AMNERIS

I pray for thy peace,...beloved, lifeless body;
May Isis, placated, receive you into Heaven!
Peace, I implore of you!
Peace, peace, peace!

AIDA AND RADAMÈS

...O Earth, farewell, *etc.*
Heaven opens to us!

PRIESTS AND PRIESTESSES

Mighty Phtha!

PHOTO CREDITS

Aida

GIUSEPPE VERDI

LIBRETTO BY ANTONIO GHISLANZONI

COMPACT DISC ONE

Atto Secondo/Act Two/Zweiter Akt/Deuxième Acte

Atto Terzo/Act Three/Dritter Akt/Troisième Acte

3	Qui Radamès verrà!	1:30
4	O patria mia	4:50
	Aida	
5	Cie! mio padre!	1:02
6	Rivedrai le foreste imbalsamate	6.27
	Aida/Amonasro	
7	Pur ti riveggo, mia dolce Aida . . .	1:17
8	Nel fiero anelito di nuova guerra	1:42
9	Fuggiam gli ardori inospiti . . . Là, tra foreste vergin	6:21
	Radamès/Aida	
10	Ma dimmi; per qual via	3:05
	Aida/Radamès/Amonasro/Amneris/Ramfis	

Atto Quarto/Act Four/Vierter Akt/Quartrième Acte

11	L'abborrita rivale a me sfuggia	2:53
	Amneris	
12	Già i sacerdoti adunansi	7:04
13	Ohimè! morir mi sento!	2:20
	Amneris	
14	Spirito del Nume	5:05
15	A lui vivo, la tomba! . . . Sacerdoti: compiste un delitto!	3:15
	Ramfis/Sacerdoti/Amneris	
16	La fatal pietra sovra me si chiuse	4:21
	Radamès/Aida	
17	Vedi? Di morte l'angelo . . . Immenso Fthà	1:39
	Aida/Sacerdotesse/Sacerdoti/Radamès	
18	O terra, addio	5:17
	Aida/Radamès/Coro/Amneris